Place, Time and Society 8-13: Curriculum Planning in History, Geography and Social Science

Place, Time and Society 8-13: Curriculum Planning in History, Geography and Social Science

Professor Alan Blyth
Keith Cooper
Ray Derricott
Gordon Elliott
Hazel Sumner
Allan Waplington

Collins·ESL Bristol
for the Schools Council

History, Geography and Social Science 8–13
This Schools Council Project was based at the School of
Education of the University of Liverpool from 1971 to
1975.

Project Team
Director: Professor Alan Blyth
Associate Director: Ray Derricott
Senior Research Officer, Geography: Gordon Elliott
Senior Research Officer, History: Allan Waplington
Senior Research Officer, Social Science: Hazel Sumner
Evaluator: Keith Cooper

First published 1976
Schools Council Publications 1976
ISBN 0 00 380002 4
Printed in Great Britain
Collins Clear-Type Press

Contents

Preface

This is the basic publication from the Schools Council Project on History, Geography and Social Science 8-13. It is written for teachers, for it is on teachers that curriculum planning depends.

The book itself is written jointly by five members of the Project Team. In practice, each part of it was prepared by one of them and then searchingly, though constructively criticised and scrutinised by all the others including the sixth member, the Evaluator, who has also contributed a section on assessment and another on variations in teachers' approach. It was also constantly tested against the reactions of groups of teachers and others—mainly teachers, as is appropriate in the circumstances—and in consequence it would be impossible to say just how often each part has been revised before publication.

In the process of this revision the Project Team, and especially its Director, were eventually cured of their tendency to introduce references designed rather to establish the Project's credentials among other writers on curriculum development than to help teachers directly. Consequently, the references that remain are comparatively few, and selected because they may be of assistance to teachers actively engaged in developing curricula for themselves. There are some other general references in the Appendixes. As for the Project's academic credentials, these must depend on the articles written by the Team in various journals. Many teachers will be more concerned about the Project's practical value. This is the particular purpose emphasised in *Curriculum planning*.

It is hoped that *Curriculum planning* will give rise to lively discussion and controversy. As is indicated in Part 3, this discussion and controversy ought to continue after the Project ends. However, the Team hope, as individuals, to continue to take an interest in what happens after that. Unlike that other Merseyside development team, the Beatles, they can still be found through their former address: School of Education, University of Liverpool, P.O. Box 147, Liverpool, L69 3BX.

There, in skylighted accommodation once occupied by the domestics who had waited upon successive Bishops of Liverpool, the Project Team worked for four memorable years. During these years, their efforts were notably facilitated by Mr John Vaughan, tutor-librarian in the University of Liverpool Education Library and his colleagues. The Team were also loyally supported by the Project's secretarial staff—Mrs Joan Edwards, Mrs Betty McMinn, Mrs Pamela Toan, Mrs Hazell Hughes, Mrs Janet Clayton, Mrs L. M. Bowe, Mrs B. D. Kerr, and Miss Pauline Dutton, as well as being tolerated, encouraged, searchingly scrutinised and enormously helped by their colleagues in the School of Education and elsewhere.

Their thanks are also due to:

The University of Liverpool for acting as grant-holder.

Many other Schools Council Projects for their friendly advice.

The Project's own Consultative Committee for its informal and unflagging interest.

The Project's Consultants and Associates for their willing assistance.

And most of all to:

The Schools Council itself and its committees, officers and secretariat for the impressive financial and administrative support which they tendered to the Project throughout the four years of its official life.

The teachers and advisers, administrators, wardens and lecturers, whose active and sincere help alone made the schools and diffusion trials possible.

Their own families, wives, husband and children without whose patient toleration of the Project's heavy, urgent, and occasionally bizarre demands it would have been impossible to achieve anything at all.

Introduction: an approach to curriculum planning

Each situation is unique

This Project Team elected, from the outset, to look at the curriculum in its relation to particular *children, teachers, schools* and *environments*. In one sense, any curriculum development project has to do this, but in the case of History, Geography and Social Science 8-13 it was always made clear that this was to be a central feature of the Project's strategy. One consequence of this decision was that no single syllabus or kit or set of materials could be produced, for each situation is unique, and requires a programme designed specifically for it. Instead, the continuing development of the curriculum must depend on the launching, within each unique situation, of a process of curriculum planning which would include the establishment of aims, the development of programmes of work (or syllabuses) and the making of appropriate materials.

Since each situation is thus regarded as unique, it is necessary to give some attention to the four aspects of these situations already mentioned, which make up its uniqueness: children, teachers, schools and environments. These the Project Team came to describe as 'the four variables'. This term is admittedly not quite accurate; a research worker would probably think of variables as something much more precise. Yet no more suitable term has emerged by which they can be denoted. Since they all figure so prominently in the Project's thinking, a brief comment will be made about each of them.

Children

There is no need to emphasise that children are a 'variable' in this sense. Each child differs in many ways from all the others, and each child differs from time to time too. Yet when children are with teachers in schools, they do develop

13

some cohesion as classes, vertical groups, tutor groups, and in other formal and informal groupings, and it is as groups that teachers usually meet them. Moreover, they share to some extent a common experience over a period of time, both inside school and outside in their home environment, and this is an important part of the basis on which any curriculum planning must rest. It is important for teachers to know not only what particular children can do and what they like doing, but also what they have done.

When a teacher encounters a group of children for the first time, he has to size them up. Experienced teachers know what to look for. One set of clues arises from their behaviour. If the children appear generally purposive, accustomed to handling books and to finding things out for themselves, and able to work constructively together, then this gives some clues about the kind of new work that they could reasonably undertake. If they seem physically vigorous but unaccustomed to any form of control except through coercion, informal work can only be initiated with caution. Again, verbal skill and knowledge of a rather traditional kind, or a prevalent lack of reading competence, give further clues about where and how children can start on anything new.

A different, though related, set of clues can be found in their appearance and in what a teacher knows about their home environment. Socio-economic differences, and even more clearly, ethnic differences, are reflected in children's appearance and movements and gestures, and can suggest to perceptive teachers the nature and range of outlook that the members of a class may have, and in particular the ways in which they may perceive Man in Place, Time and Society.

However, such general impressions can be misleading. Children differ within groups more than is sometimes recognised, and there is always some individual to belie any hasty generalisation that a teacher makes about his class. In one respect, of course, individual differences have long been recognised. Children have been traditionally classified by ability (more accurately, by attainment), indeed almost too much attention has been paid to this kind of variation at the expense of other characteristics such as sociability and varieties of temperament. These other differences may remain comparatively concealed in traditional teaching but, as many teachers' experience shows, they become more exposed when the process of education itself becomes more varied and more kinds of activity are involved. This, of course, often happens when innovations in curriculum are introduced.

Of course, the whole literature on child development is in a sense relevant to children as a variable in the school situation. All that can be done here is to point out, in the simplest terms, the kinds of clues which may help teachers to estimate how this first variable may figure in any particular situation for which they are planning. But these clues may also serve a dual purpose. They may not only indicate the ways in which a class or group may respond, but also suggest how the class and its variety and experience may itself be used as a first-hand resource for learning about Man in Place, Time and Society.

Teachers

Like children, teachers also vary. They have different kinds and lengths of experience, different interests, different personalities and outlooks, different ways of reacting to children, colleagues and to society. Again, like children, teachers vary within themselves from time to time, and they, too, live in formal and informal groups which, over a period of time, develop characteristics of their own.

Just as teachers need to size up their classes, so they need to size up their colleagues and themselves as a 'variable' in the process of curriculum planning. This is a more difficult task. The 'giftie' of being able to appraise oneself, one's own weaknesses and preferences as well as one's strengths, is not a universal one, and its acquisition can be difficult. Among teachers, this may actually be more of a problem than in some other occupations because there is still a survival of the tradition that teachers should conceal their teaching, and especially their limitations, from one another. This tradition is now giving way. The growth of co-operative teaching of various kinds is likely to restrict its effect still more. However, it has not yet disappeared.

Co-operative teaching is one of the features which innovations in the curriculum may involve. It need not necessarily imply team teaching in the strict sense, but it does call for a measure of joint planning and consultation between teachers. For this purpose there is a positive value in collaboration between teachers with different interests, different ways of approaching their task, and different things that they can do well. For example, some teachers are basically subject specialists, while others have been mainly concerned with children. Some people have become teachers because they are particularly interested in the part that schools can play in the improvement of society. Other teachers show a mixture of all these characteristics. If teachers with varying outlooks as well as various competences do work together, they can support one another and reinforce one another's skills.

Schools

At first, it may seem superfluous to refer to schools in addition to teachers and children. Surely, it may appear, schools comprise teachers and children. They do; but there are also three important additional aspects of schools. For one thing, they have their own administrative status; primary, middle or secondary; county or voluntary, grammar, modern or comprehensive, and so on. In addition, they vary greatly according to sheer size. Even within the Project the schools ranged in size from under 100 to over 1,000 and no teacher needs to be told what differences this makes to what can be done and how it is done. But they are also social organisations with their own principles of cohesion, their own cultures, and their constraints, and their own relation to the organisation of the wider society. The Project Team decided quite early in their discussions that all of this made it necessary to include schools as a separate variable.

Much that has been written about schools as social and administrative units is couched in the terminology of the administrative sciences, which is not always familiar or even particularly congenial to teachers. But the reality about which it is written is certainly familiar to them. They know well enough when they are able to try out ideas that would be unthinkable in the school down the road. They are aware of when they have the backing of a sympathetic Head, or when they are suspected of intellectual arson by members of the local council. They know the frustration caused by sheer lack of capitation allowances or when they see scarce resources being steered towards some areas of the curriculum rather than others.

They even know how it can happen that their own pupils' parents, or even the pupils themselves, accustomed to routine, are the first to be shocked by innovation. Conversely, they know what chaos and uncertainty can be caused when a Head or a school staff as a whole proclaims an educational revolution without having adequately anticipated the consequences of doing so. So, when planning any new developments, teachers need to size up their situations, to take account of the opinions of others, and to act only within the limits that these indicate; or having estimated the possibilities, to change them.

Environments

The fourth 'variable' is the physical and social environment of schools. This, too, is part of the shared experience of the children and teachers, at least to some extent. It is common knowledge that it permeates schools in a number of ways. What is considered important in the environment affects what is considered important in school. Where there are two or more socially distinct parts in the environment, this is reflected in school. If the local environment is very separate and distinctive (as in some villages, for example), then the school partakes of this separateness. Even in an age of mass media and mass consumption, these differences remain detectable, more in some places than in others. No initiatives in curriculum planning can be undertaken unless these characteristics are borne in mind.

But when the part of the curriculum for which the initiative is planned is about Man in Place, Time and Society, then the environment takes on a second kind of significance also. For a subtle relationship exists between the effect of the environment on children and the study by children of the environment. They are, by learning about it, learning too about themselves. Thus it might be said without undue distortion, that the local environment is both *context* and *content* in education.

Teachers, when planning curriculum, need to think sensitively about some of the possible implications of this interrelationship. If by learning about the environment children learn about themselves, they may come to see themselves and their families and friends in a new light. Their reactions to their environment could give rise to a range of responses: anger, defensiveness, evasiveness, indifference. Teachers might also need to think of what stance they might want to take towards parents and others living in the environment, for quite basic issues might be raised, issues which would have to be differently approached according to the kind of environment in which the school finds itself.

Interaction between the 'four variables'

Children, teachers, schools and environments constantly affect each other and interact with each other. Any change effected in one of them is likely to have repercussions on the rest. Any innovation in curriculum planning that is desirable should have the effect of improving all of them. For an innovation to be successful, it depends in particular on the second and third of the four, teachers and schools. If the school variable is favourable, that is, if the conditions in the school as an institution allow teachers to plan curriculum effectively, then this enables effective innovation to be planned. The actual planning depends primarily on the teachers, with the head teacher either as an active participant or at least (as a part of the school variable) as a supporting well-wisher. These assumptions guided the Project Team in their actual work in schools and subsequently.

The Project's experimental programme in schools

The Project Team having worked out a style of approach to

18

curriculum planning, decided to formulate ideas about the particular part of the curriculum with which they were concerned; the part relating to Place, Time and Society for children aged 8 - 13. These ideas are embodied in the rest of the book. They had next to be tried out in practice, in as wide a range as possible of schools catering for children aged 8 - 13. Thirty schools were chosen, and in these the Team worked alongside teachers for over a year (1972-73), developing the Project's general ideas and trying out various practical approaches. The Team was able to support these experimental schemes of work with materials for teachers and children. The saga of this experimental programme cannot be told within the compass of this book, but that programme constitutes the Project's guarantee. The ideas and suggestions embodied in this volume have stood the test of that practical experience.

The Project's diffusion programme

The Project's ideas have been further tested in a different way. If each situation is unique, it follows that a major responsibility for curriculum planning must rest on the second of the 'four variables', the teachers. Consequently, a further programme was launched in 1973, a diffusion programme during which teachers and Local Education Authorities were approached, in different ways, to find which would be the most effective means of establishing a continuing process of curriculum planning after the Project had ended.

To begin with, it was necessary to take some action to ensure the continuity would be preserved even in the schools and L.E.A.s in which the experimental programme itself had been conducted. In addition, a limited number of new initiatives were launched in different types of area. Here, as in the experimental programme in schools, the outcome led to the modification of the Team's original ideas and, it is hoped, to a realistic appraisal of what is practicable. This diffusion programme, made possible by a generous extension of the Project's grant, is the basis for the suggestions made in Part 3.

The plan of the book

This Introduction has indicated the approach to curriculum planning which guided the Project Team in their work, and which led to the view that the process, not the materials, of curriculum development is what matters. There is indeed a place for materials; the Project has issued a very extensive collection of materials. But the outcome of greatest importance is the process of curriculum planning and its impact on children.

The book is divided into three Parts, each subdivided into sections. Part 1 is concerned with the Project's area of the curriculum - History, Geography and the Social Sciences as they relate to children aged 8 to 13. Part 2 is the heart of the book, for it suggests how teachers might actually set about planning work for themselves, preferably in groups in schools or teachers' centres. In conclusion, Part 3 suggests how the process launched in such groups may be helped to continue in a self-perpetuating way.

Curriculum planning does not blandly ignore the problems of everyday life in schools. Neither does it offer ready answers. Schools are not places in which there are any ready answers. The only people who can find answers suited to particular children in particular schools in particular environments are the particular teachers concerned, and they will only find the answers as they live within the situation. The Project Team hope that this book will help them to find their own answers, and believe that those are the only answers with which they will, or should, be satisfied.

Part 1 Subjects and curriculum planning

Part 1 is about the study of Man in Place, Time and Society and how this element can figure in the curriculum for children between the ages of 8 and 13. The first two sections are of a rather general nature, raising some questions that the Project has found particularly important, and in those sections the area of study will still be referred to as Man in Place, Time and Society, the designation that the Project Team devised for itself. But the Project's real title is History, Geography and Social Science 8-13 and in section 1.3, for the first time, subjects as such are introduced. Some attention is given to what a subject is and how it is related to academic disciplines as resources. Then geography, history and social science are discussed in turn, so that the specific value and contribution of each can be considered.

1.1 A necessary part of the curriculum

The inclusion of any subject or group of subjects in the curriculum requires justification. Why should teachers expect the study of Man in Place, Time and Society to take up any part - let alone a significant part - of the child's time at school? There are two main areas in which some justification must be attempted. One arises from our idea of what counts as *education* and *being educated* in our society today, the other takes into account the needs of the pupils.

Our present society exhibits a concern for the welfare and dignity of mankind which is historically unprecedented. We would be unlikely to admit as a truly educated person anyone who did not, to some degree at least, show this concern. The embodiment of this in the school curriculum is, in part, related to moral and aesthetic education. At least as important, however, is the study of human variety and human achievement which has traditionally been the concern of history and geography, together perhaps with more recent developments such as social studies or environmental studies. Perhaps the point is best made in the negative. Is it possible to talk of someone as being educated if he has no conception of the past, no awareness of the world around him, and no understanding of the workings of human society? If such a conception is not possible, then we are clearly entitled, if not mandated, to include such study in our curriculum.

There is another aspect of being an educated person which is relevant here; the ability, and the desire, to play an active part in the life of the society. It seems possible that the desire to play such a part can be stimulated by the study of Man in Place, Time and Society; it is surely undeniable that the ability to do so will, in terms of the school curriculum, be brought out almost exclusively in this study. An acquaintance with, and some understanding of, the society's past; an awareness of the relationships of the society to its location on the earth's surface; and an understanding of the processes at work within the society, are all necessary conditions for a full participation in the life of the society. It should perhaps be made clear that this formulation is as relevant to a desire to change society as it is to a desire to preserve it.

Some consideration will be given later, in the sections considering history, geography and the social sciences separately, to the particular needs of children which can be met through the study of each subject. There is, however, a more basic consideration which is common to all of these subjects, one which arises from their concern with Man. People, and children in particular, need to be able to build a realistic image of themselves in relation to others. It is this in particular which comes to mind in the dictum that the proper study of mankind is Man. Only by looking at other people past and present, their struggles, their hopes and fears, their responses as individuals and as part of a group, can the child develop his image of himself, and his values and beliefs. Much of his observation will be of the people around him, whether at home or at school. Part of what the school can accomplish in this area, however, is to encourage among children the practice of observing people with whom they are not in constant interaction, in a situation of which they are not part, and by which they are not threatened. Whether this experience is literary, historical, geographical or illuminated through the social sciences, the need for it is, and must always be, great.

Those who plan a curriculum can meet this need most effectively if they ensure that these various modes of experience are suitably blended within it.

1.2 Values and issues

Any justification for the inclusion of a subject-area in a curriculum depends basically on the adoption of recognisable values. There is no such thing as neutrality in this respect. To expose children in any way to one set of experiences rather than another is to select from the range of possible experiences, and this selection must be on a basis of values. Even the brief introductory claim for studying Man in Place, Time and Society set out in the preceding section embodies some element of value-judgement and value-selection.

The Project Team took the view from the outset that they had to be explicit about this. They were, therefore, involved at an early stage in deciding what range of values they were prepared to accept and to encourage in others, and also what values they would regard as unacceptable and would be prepared to discourage.

Two values emerged as basic to the Project's thinking and intentions. The first of these was that each person and each culture has its own claim to legitimate existence and that, therefore, education ought not to be based on the assumptions that some persons and some cultures are superior to others. Instead, it should enable children to develop their own ways of looking at individuals and cultures and their own criteria for deciding which, if any, are preferable in their eyes. This implies in turn the second basic value, namely that children should be actively initiated into the discussion of problems and issues in society rather than being shielded from problems, or being taught about problems as though there were always 'right' answers, like the answers to be found at the back of traditional textbooks in mathematics.

These two values have consequences for curriculum

development which merit attention. They concern teachers in several ways.

One of these is the way in which teachers look upon children. There has been a tendency to assume that children between the ages of 8 and 13 are not ready for the open discussion of social issues, that they lack the necessary experience or even the necessary emotional maturity and stability. The experience of the Project does not uphold this view. Rather, it suggests that children engage readily in controversial topics, including topics relating to their own situation. After a period of adjustment to the novelty, as it often is, of undertaking the study of problems in school, they appreciate a teacher who is willing to explore these problems with them rather than one who imposes some form of taboo on controversy. In fact, their capabilities are often much greater than has usually been expected. The one way in which their comparative immaturity does necessarily limit the exploration of such issues is the complexity of the ideas involved[1]. For example, it is easier for children to study their own reactions to one another as a group than to puzzle over an international monetary crisis, even though the former issue may well make greater emotional demands on them as individual participants in the situation.

A second implication of the Project's basic values for teachers is that they need to come to terms with the essentially controversial nature of any study of Man in Place, Time and Society. Whereas it may be possible to select, within the fields of science and mathematics, topics and problems which are relatively 'safe' to handle, it is scarcely possible to defuse the study of Man, except by confining children to quaint trivialities or by attempting to conduct teaching in a dogmatic way which is incompatible with the Project's values.

The active stimulation of discussion about important issues related to the past and present diversity of mankind is virtually bound to raise questions to which there is no one right answer, but about which people can and do disagree strongly. Some of these questions are explored in the Project's published units, but there are many others which are likely to arise with particular children, teachers, schools and environments. Moreover, as schools and environments become socially more diverse, following the abolition of selection in secondary education and the emergence of a multi-cultural society, it is increasingly probable that any group of children will differ sharply among themselves about these controversial issues.

It is not only among children that controversial issues raise questions of policy for teachers. The school and environment variables are also involved. Some schools are organised in such a way that the mere raising of controversial issues with children might lead to reprimand for the teacher. Some environments could involve similar consequences from parents, governors, administrators and others for the school as a whole. This can happen irrespective of the social or political character of the environment itself.

To enable himself to handle the value-laden issues involved in any study of Man in Place, Time and Society, a teacher has finally to develop a certain measure of confidence in his own values, and of competence in organising work of this nature with children[2], and of readiness to defend his own courses of action while bearing in mind the rights and susceptibilities of others and the realistic limits of what is possible. All of this requires also an increasing degree of professional maturity and autonomy, and this, as the Project Team came to realise, amounts to a third value running through the Project's strategy as a whole, re-emphasising the basic significance of the teacher variable. It can perhaps be linked with the previous two by saying that one of the Project's major aims is to develop the autonomy of children through the autonomy of the teacher[3].

There is one further implication of this approach to the values and issues involved in a study of Man in Place, Time and Society. The exploration of problems and the encouragement of children to develop their own systems of values and preferences calls for a particular emphasis in the actual programme of work undertaken in schools. For it is not enough to proclaim this as a policy; there must be some means of implementing it. The experience of the Project in schools eventually led the team to select two qualities which seemed particularly appropriate for this purpose, namely *critical thinking* and *empathy*.

The meaning of critical thinking is fairly self-evident, though it is perhaps worthwhile to emphasise that it includes both the capacity, and the readiness, to examine situations and problems, and also values and beliefs, in an unbiased way. Obviously this is a capacity that requires a long time to develop, and indeed one which can never be fully attained, though a start can be made during and before the middle years.

Empathy is a little less obvious because it is sometimes confused with sympathy. Its meaning, as used by the Project, is the capacity to understand the point of view of others without necessarily agreeing with it, and, as it were, to be able temporarily to act the part of another person. Both of these qualities are the concern of the curriculum as a whole, and indeed of education as a whole, but they are especially needed for a study of Man in Place, Time and Society. In addition, as suggested in section 2.1, the study of Place, Time and Society can be a means of developing them.

The development of these qualities could, perhaps should, have another kind of significance. A child, or an adolescent, or an adult, who has learned to practise critical thinking and empathy has gained more than a pair of necessary tools for the study of society. He has also acquired a part of the equipment required for living as a citizen of a democratic society. It is difficult to develop this point further without going into much greater depth than is possible here. But it is worth while at least to suggest that a person versed in critical thinking and empathy will be more likely to behave in a rational manner, more likely to understand his own motives and impulses, more likely to realise that force is often a poor way of trying to solve social problems. He is also more likely to be ready to acknowledge and assert that real problems exist and cannot be swept aside. The Project Team do not expect that their values will result in the rapid spread of ideal democratic behaviour; but they do hope that the Project's influence will at least result in some modest movement in that direction.

References
1 Here, perhaps, is the only point at which the thought

and experimentation of Piaget and his school has a direct implication for the study of Man in Place, Time and Society.

2 The Humanities Curriculum Project directed by Lawrence Stenhouse has placed great emphasis on the development of such skills among teachers. The most accessible short summary of the H.C.P.'s approach is probably to be found in *The Humanities Project: an Introduction*, London, Heineman Educational, 1970.

3 A standard advocacy of autonomy as an aim for the education of younger children is presented in Dearden, R. F., *The Philosophy of Primary Education*, London, Routledge and Kegan Paul, 1968.

1.3 Disciplines as resources

A terminology for the discussion of subjects and disciplines
The study of Man in Place, Time and Society depends necessarily on resources of knowledge and skills which have been built up over the years. Claims have often been advanced that children should be discoverers of their own selves and their own place in the world, but these were never intended to mean that they or their teachers should do so without reference to the vast store of resources which others have already accumulated and classified[1]. This store of resources is subdivided into areas usually known in schools as *subjects*.

In higher education they are known more distinctively as *disciplines*, a term which has a double significance because it implies both that they organise knowledge in a disciplined way and that anyone who aspires to undertake high-level study and research in one of these fields, as a lifelong vocation, must undergo a stringent form of discipline before being allowed to do so. To distinguish disciplines from subjects, and for no other reason, disciplines will henceforth be given capitals and subjects will appear in lower-case letters[2].

The study of Man in Place, Time and Society in schools looks in particular to the disciplines of History and Geography, and a further group of disciplines including Economics, Sociology, Social Anthropology, Social Psychology and Political Science, which can justifiably be called Social Sciences. Other disciplines such as Architecture and Archaeology are closely, but not quite so closely, relevant. It is these disciplines, especially the first two, which have provided the material distilled or otherwise transmitted for use in schools.

Consequently, the titles of these disciplines have themselves figured as subjects in the programmes of schools, especially secondary schools. Schools too have taught history and geography, though after these and a little economics the list has usually thinned out. Meanwhile in primary, and now in middle and some secondary schools, the notion of subjects has been challenged and in their place there now usually appears something broader, such as social studies or environmental studies or humanities or integrated studies. Thus it cannot be assumed that there is a simple relationship between disciplines in higher education and subjects in the curriculum of schools. Again, the thought-processes involved in both are similar; but there is a different emphasis in the subject-matter. Indeed, teachers who have studied one or more of the disciplines in their own higher education have frequently found that they needed to learn whole topics in the school subjects that were relatively new to them. Topics, such as transport or costume or the human details of farming, which are of marginal interest to the academic disciplines have been found centrally important in the programmes of many schools.

This, then, is the way in which the individual disciplines and subjects will be considered in the rest of the book. The distinction between the two has been slightly overdrawn, to simplify the discussion that follows. It should be emphasised that no ambitious claims are made on its behalf; but it does have some basis in reality. Finally, to complete the terminology to be used, it is necessary to find some way of denoting the whole range of disciplines and subjects concerned with the Project's curricular area, the study of Man in Place, Time and Society. For this purpose the disciplines will be collectively termed *the social disciplines*, and the

28

subjects will be given the useful designation devised by the Scots, *the social subjects*. The last term seems more appropriate for the Project's purposes than 'environmental studies' or 'social studies' or 'humanities' or 'integrated studies', since it denotes their scope without suggesting other subjects, or ways of organising the curriculum. Here again, no claim is made for the suitability of these collective terms except that they will help the discussion in this book.

The terminology as a whole is summarised in figure 1.

Fig 1

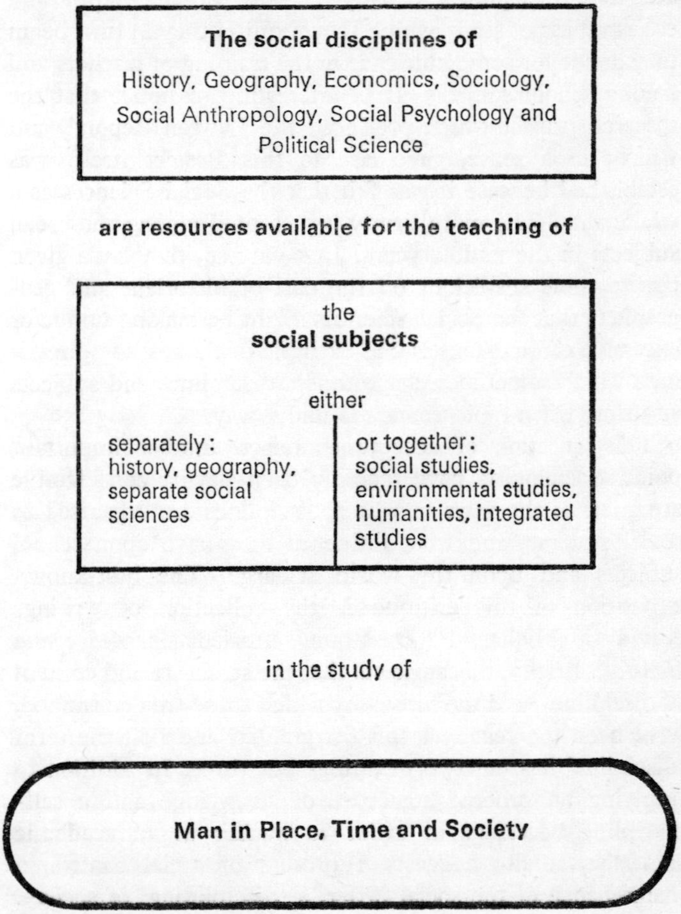

The social disciplines of

History, Geography, Economics, Sociology, Social Anthropology, Social Psychology and Political Science

---

are resources available for the teaching of

---

the
social subjects

either

| separately:
history, geography,
separate social
sciences | or together:
social studies,
environmental studies,
humanities, integrated
studies |

---

in the study of

Man in Place, Time and Society

Some characteristics of subjects and disciplines

With the help of this terminology, it will be worth while to look a little further at the nature of these disciplines and subjects generally, before the contributions of each are considered.

First, it is important to remember that neither disciplines, nor subjects, are something essential to the human mind[3], persisting unchanged over the centuries. For example, all the social disciplines are of comparatively recent origin, and one or two of the Social Sciences are very recent indeed. As they become admitted to the family of credit-worthy academic disciplines, usually because of the depth and cohesiveness of study which they require, they in turn begin to clamour for some influence in the training of teachers and among school subjects. It is interesting to notice that the research project which produced the Lawton Report[4], and which, in a sense, gave rise to this Project itself, was established because it was felt that the Social Sciences as a whole should be more firmly represented among the social subjects in the middle years. In saying so, they have given rise to some suspicions on the part of historians and geographers that the Social Sciences might be making undue or excessive claims. This is one example of the jostling uneasiness which sometimes characterises disciplines and subjects at a time when rapid change is under way.

This question of acceptance raises another important point. Sociologists have recently been paying considerable attention to the ways in which disciplines are organised as social systems, and what influence they have upon school subjects and upon the world at large. The best-known exposition of this critique is the collection of writings edited by Michael F. D. Young entitled *Knowledge and Control*[5]. Briefly, this suggests that the structure and content of disciplines, and the means by which these are determined, have been too readily taken for granted and that the term 'discipline' has not two meanings but three. In addition to implying an ordered structure of knowledge and a self-discipline necessary in order to qualify as an academic specialist, it also suggests a process of social control, a maintenance of the social order, a 'disciplining' of society.

30

Thus, historians, for example, can decide not only what is necessary to become an historian, but also what history should be included in a public examination which must be taken by those who aspire to enter the corridors of power.

In this way they play some part in deciding what sort of knowledge counts in society. If this knowledge is more open through subjects to some people than to others, because of the way in which it is presented, then this can in itself affect the composition of the leadership in society. It would of course be unfair to suggest that historians are particularly prone to exercise this form of social control. Geographers, economists, psychologists and anthropologists do it too, while sociologists and political scientists may well catch themselves red-handed, and perhaps also red-faced, practising in their own disciplines, albeit in a rather different mode, the very procedures that they are busy exposing in others.

It may at first appear that these processes are of little relevance to the middle years of schooling because they seem to be concerned more specifically with public examinations. This is not so, because the social disciplines influence the social subjects, and in any case public examinations cast long shadows before them, affecting how teachers think about syllabuses and curriculum for children below the age of 13.

What is more, this view of disciplines has a significance not only for subjects in school, but also for school organisation in general. As Bernstein points out in one of the most celebrated chapters in *Knowledge and Control*[6], a school with a subject curriculum closely derived from the disciplines (he uses the term 'collection paradigm') is likely to determine closely, from quite an early age, what parts of the social subjects, and other subjects, children should learn. It is also likely to sort its pupils out through a carefully planned procedure, on the evidence of individual attainment in particular subjects. Only later, when they have passed this test of competence in those subjects, it allows them some share in choosing what knowledge they should pursue. On the other hand, a school with an integrated approach to subjects, for example, one which treats the social subjects as a unity (following the 'integration paradigm') is much more likely to allow children to explore knowledge freely and collectively without limitation to particular subjects. It may pay for this freedom by sacrificing the stability and pre-dictability and control mechanisms which a subject-based curriculum and its attendant procedures imparts to a school.

No quick summary of Bernstein's views can begin to do justice to the close reasoning of his arguments, but some reference, however brief, to his comments on subjects and integration is necessary in any reference to curriculum planning, for all such planning must come to terms with the nature of disciplines and of subjects and with their impact within schools.

The Project's view of subjects and disciplines

All of these considerations were borne in mind by the Project Team when they developed their own views about subjects. They decided that the most justifiable approach would be to regard the social disciplines as primarily *resources*, resources not only of information but, more importantly, resources of methods and skills and of ways of looking at Man in Place, Time and Society. Clearly this is a much broader use of the term 'resource' than is associated with a resources centre or even with resource-based learning. It means nothing less than the availability of the accumulated achievements of the disciplines themselves.

This view of disciplines embodies several advantages. For one thing, their distinctiveness can be retained whether they contribute to the school curriculum directly through the individual social subjects or in some other way. Again, this view takes account of those valuable and useful books and materials, belonging to the social subjects, which are available in schools. They embody, as the Project's own publications are intended to do, the outcome of scholarship in the social disciplines as applied to the needs of schools. It does not, however, countenance any approach to the social subjects which is based only on common knowledge and which ignores the specific contribution of the social disciplines.

In addition, this conception of disciplines assists the abandonment of a view of subjects as a body of content that must be absorbed. The very fact that the disciplines constitute the available resources makes this point clear. It may be possible, in a tedious and diluted fashion, to try to 'cover' a school subject, though to the children this may be a rather meaningless procedure. But nobody can even contemplate 'covering' a discipline in a lifetime, still less in the years between 8 and 13. At the same time, the emphasis placed by the Project on each discipline as a resource affords some likelihood that none of them will be overlooked or elbowed out. Therefore, in relation to any one topic, a wide and stimulating range of knowledge and skills and perspectives can be brought into use together. This is what the Project means when referring to the use of the disciplines in *interrelation*.

This term was originally devised to bring out the value of the combined contributions of the disciplines without implying that they should be merged into some synthetic and perhaps shapeless whole. The Project Team were very concerned to retain and to respect their distinctiveness without merely considering each discipline in isolation. Like others who have faced similar issues in the curriculum, and have frankly considered the implications of an integrated curriculum[7], the Project Team have always insisted on the importance of the separate disciplines as contributors, bearing in mind that they themselves are, as academic studies, in fact interrelated, and their separate strengths gain from this mutual awareness and support.

For, as others have insisted[8], integration involves having something to integrate, at any rate in the mind of the teacher. An analogy might be taken from nutrition. Even if the children eat their meals as integrated wholes, the mother or whoever prepares them has to know and recognise the individual ingredients and see them in interrelation. So it is with the curriculum. However much children exercise their spontaneous curiosity on life as a whole, their teachers need to know something about the use of the disciplines if they are to give the children the opportunity of extending their interests meaningfully and productively. To take an example from the social subjects: children out looking at local buildings may notice a contrast between two sorts of house. If a teacher recognises that they are of different ages and that this is a clue to the growth of a village or a town as a part of the national story, then the children's awareness can be much more fully developed. Yet in order to be able to do this, the teacher has to know not just how to classify domestic architecture by periods[9] but also how to interpret contrasts in domestic architecture in relation to other kinds of knowledge, which in turn requires knowing something about History as such. At the same time the location of the houses, and the way of life and work of the people who lived and live in them, requires also knowing something from Geography and the Social Sciences. It is the readiness to know which discipline to draw on, how, and for what purposes, that constitutes using the disciplines in interrelation.

The range of available intellectual resources may for particular purposes be further extended beyond the bounds of the social disciplines themselves to include, for instance, examples from the literary disciplines or the sciences, or books and other sources outside the scope of any discipline.

These include personal sources. One of the striking features about the study of Man in Place, Time and Society is that some of the most pertinent material lies outside disciplines and subjects altogether, in the accumulated experience of men and women who in their work or their leisure have acquired astonishingly full knowledge about a locality or about some particular kind of economic activity with which they have been concerned: an industrial process perhaps, or the commodities conveyed by a particular road haulage concern.

The last point might appear paradoxical. For it seems odd that if the disciplines as resources are so important, it can also be important to consider resources that lie outside them. The explanation of the paradox is that these additional resources can only be of value if they are interpreted through the disciplines themselves. It might be hard to find the particular information about the contents of the lorries and the actual industrial processes, previously mentioned, by searching in the standard textbooks about the disciplines, or even in books catering specifically for school subjects. Yet, without the structure and skills and methodologies of those disciplines, the significance of such supplementary personal information would be largely overlooked.

34

Learning to use the disciplines

Teachers who have not had any sort of formal apprenticeship in the social disciplines may well be worried about what is involved in using these disciplines as resources. However, they are not required to become scholars in the individual disciplines; they are required to become *mediators*, with sufficient knowledge to draw on the disciplines. This is a distinctive part of their professional role. This involves, at least, being aware of the main ways in which geographers, historians and social scientists go about their work, so that they can start asking some of the important questions raised by practitioners of the disciplines. In this way, teachers can learn more about both the processes and the main ideas characteristic of the disciplines in the course of devising work for, and ideally with, children. Sometimes indeed, even in this early phase of using the disciplines, they can begin to convey to the children in their turn some idea of these processes and ideas and of their significance (see section 2.2).

This minimum level of awareness is not a level at which teachers will be happy to operate for long. It is, however, enough to make it worth starting. It has been part of the task of the Project to try to provide some help for teachers when they want to learn more for themselves about the social disciplines. In each of the published units, for instance, the material has been written and structured in such a way that the contribution of the disciplines becomes clear in the teacher's guide to the unit. A teacher working through a unit with the guide would be able to exemplify in a number of ways the relationship between the contribution of the disciplines and classroom practice. Another section of the Project's publications - the support booklets, notably *Using sources and resources* and *Using social statistics*, also offer help in this way. The chapters on the individual disciplines in this book and the references included in them, would also make a helpful starting-point, especially if it were supplemented by a shrewd and insightful use of good recent resource books prepared for children[10].

Where these individual disciplines are concerned, it seems likely that teachers will in general be more unhappy with the prospect of handling processes or ideas related to the Social

Sciences than those associated with History and Geography. After all, most of us did some sort of history and geography at school, even if it needs some updating. There is, however, more expertise available for learning about the Social Sciences than teachers may realise. For example, numbers of teachers have studied the Social Science Foundation Course for an Open University degree. Often this is seen as a part of the teacher's life which is quite separate from the classroom. Yet, it is both possible and satisfying for a teacher to use such knowledge in a teaching situation. It may even help him to understand it better.

Similarly, there are areas of the courses in the Sociology of Education and the Psychology of Education as taught in the teacher's initial training and in-service courses which do not just illuminate the process of education but can provide classroom material and ideas. As indicated in the Introduction, the Project regards the social environment as an essential part both of the context of education and of the content of education. It appears entirely appropriate, that some of what teachers know about the children's situation and potential should be increasingly shared with the children themselves as their insight into themselves in their social world develops.

The Project itself gained valuable experience of these possibilities in the course of the schools programme and it was encouraging to see how the teachers concerned became increasingly confident in handling material about families, group behaviour and topics from Sociology and Social Psychology which they had previously associated with knowledge about children, but which they now saw also as potential knowledge and experience for children. Section 3.2 suggests some ways in which other teachers could be helped to make this kind of use of their own professional expertise.

Subjects or integration: a note
The Project Team have often been asked to declare themselves 'for' or 'against' the integration of the curriculum. In practice, it is not possible or justifiable to make a simple, universally-applicable choice, and in any case the Team believe that the most important point is that irrespective of

the structure of the curriculum as a whole, the disciplines should be used as resources in interrelation. Nevertheless, it is possible to say something also about the question of integration.

As children grow older, they do appear increasingly able to apprehend the point and purpose of different subjects. Schools can impede, or control, this capacity. But it does not depend entirely on school. A parallel trend can be seen in their leisure pursuits in which they become increasingly dissatisfied with undifferentiated activities and seek to organise and categorise what they do. As they become keen on particular kinds of activity, they also come to appreciate the value of experts who can offer them guidance and help arising from prolonged experience and skill acquisition.

This aspect of children's development coincides also, of course, with the increasing proximity of public examinations and thus with a new kind of valuation of subjects for them, their parents and their teachers. But, the appreciation of the value of separate fields of study does not rest solely on their instrumental utility for examination purposes. Thus, to some extent, the differentiation of the curriculum in the later middle years can be justified in terms of children's development.

On the other hand, as Bernstein has hinted, this differentiation also has social implications. The progressive division of the curriculum into separate parts as children grow older could be regarded as a means of maintaining the existing order in both school and society. The change to an integrated curriculum might therefore have far-reaching social consequences. This hypothesis has not yet been investigated in detail[11], but many who look to education as an agent of social change would endorse it, even if this appears to run counter to the argument based on children's own development.

Weighing these considerations as well as their own distinctive approach, the Project Team would tentatively suggest that:

1 In junior or middle schools, the age-band 8 to 9 is the point at which the specific contribution of the social subjects within the curriculum should be introduced. This

can be either as a 'broad area' given a specific place in the programme, or part of a topic-based approach to a curriculum that continues to be mainly integrated (or rather, one which has not begun to be mainly differentiated), provided that the contribution of the social disciplines is given adequate weight within the programme as a whole.

2 Between 9 and 11, in junior or middle schools, the case for looking at the 'broad area' of the social subjects as a separate concern becomes stronger, but not unanswerable. It is still possible to maintain a mainly integrated approach but it is more difficult to cater within it adequately for the rapid increase in intellectual and social development of the children and for their individual interests.

3 Between 11 and 13, in middle or secondary schools, the social subjects as a whole should be given a distinctive place in the curriculum, even though their boundary might not coincide exactly with history, geography and social science. But the question now is whether, within this broad area, the individual subjects should themselves be separately introduced. With growing flexibility and diversity in schools and society, and increasing demands for adaptability, there is a strong case for maintaining some form of integration and interaction between the social subjects up to the age of 13, but, at the same time, for facing shrewdly and humanely the social consequences of doing so.

This point of view may well be viewed with suspicion by those who regard subjects as, essentially, bodies of prescribed content. As has already been emphasised, the Project Team reject this view of what school subjects are for. The use of disciplines as resources is quite a different matter from the use of subjects as defined, specified, irreducible content. Even in situations where separate subjects are taught, the Project maintains that they should be viewed rather as ways of learning and forms of awareness.

The Project Team consider, then, that for a typical school pattern with the age of transfer at 11, 12 or 13, a suitable framework for the social subjects would be one which placed rather less emphasis on individual subjects as such, between

11 and 13, than is usually found in secondary schools. This resembles to some extent the general guidelines suggested in the Lawton Report[12]. However, this pattern of curriculum is only intended for a typical school situation. In each particular set of circumstances, the four variables have to be taken into account for this purpose as well as others. Judging from the Project's experience, it may often be wiser to adhere for a short time to a subject-based syllabus throughout a secondary or even the upper part of a middle school, or to prolong to the age of 11 or beyond the undifferentiated curriculum of a junior school, than to embark precipitately on a course of change, however laudable that course may sound, thereby running the risk of jeopardising the whole process. The implications of change must be thought out very carefully in advance, with Bernstein's comments and others in mind (see section 3.1).

Whatever may be the solution in particular situations, it remains true that if disciplines are perceived as resources rather than as defined and mandatory bodies of subject-matter, they can never be the tyrants of the curriculum. Nor should they. Their exponents should not claim, as they sometimes try to do, a unique educative value for separate subjects in isolation, each derived from a discipline and equipped with an irreducible core of content, simply by asserting that their value is self-evident. What they can, and legitimately should, claim is that without the disciplines as resources, and without some idea of their scope, approach and fascination, any curriculum is deprived of its most significant basis. If they assert this, while leaving the actual organisation of the curriculum to schools, there is no reason why that should not accommodate the reasonable claims of scholars and teachers alike.

Each of the social disciplines has its own characteristic contribution to make; in fact, its own scope, approach and fascination. The next three sections indicate the nature of these contributions.

References
1 This question is briefly discussed in Blyth, W. A. L. 'Discovering Time, Place and Society'. *Education 3-13*, 1/2,

Collins, 1973, pp. 69-74.

2 For a discussion of some issues related to disciplines, see Whitfield, R. C. (ed.) *The Disciplines of the Curriculum*, London, McGraw Hill, 1971, especially the ways in which the claims of individual disciplines are related to the general issues raised by Whitfield himself. Some further questions important for a deeper study of this topic are raised in Schwab, J. J. (ed.) *The Structure of Knowledge and the Curriculum*. Chicago, Rand McNally, 1964.

3 In current debates about the structure of knowledge it is of course maintained by Paul Hirst and others that there are fundamental *forms* of knowledge, or 'realms of meaning'; but nobody maintains that these are equivalent to subjects.

4 Lawton, D., Campbell, J. and Burkitt, V. *Social Studies 8-13*, Schools Council Working Paper No. 39. London, Evans/Methuen Educational, 1971.

5 Young, Michael F. D. *Knowledge and Control: New Directions for the Sociology of Education*. London, Collier-Macmillan, 1971.

6 Bernstein, Basil, 'On the classification and framing of educational knowledge' in Young, Michael F. D., *op. cit.*

7 It is not suggested that this belittling of the disciplines has been advocated by curriculum development projects concerned with integration. Indeed, in the area of the social subjects, both Lawrence Stenhouse for the Humanities Curriculum Project, and David Bolam for the Keele Integrated Studies Project, have been at pains to emphasise the basic importance of individual disciplines for their particular purposes. See Stenhouse, L. A. 'Some limitations of the use of objectives in curriculum research and planning'. *Paedagogica Europaea* 6, 1970-71, pp. 73-83 and Bolam, D. 'Integration in the curriculum: a case-study in the humanities', *ibid.* pp. 157-171. (See also *Exploration Man: an Introduction to Integrated Studies*, Schools Council Integrated Studies Project. London, Oxford Univ. Press, 1972, pp. 10-11.) But this point has sometimes been overlooked in general discussions about integrated curricula.

8 See for example Pring, Richard, 'Curriculum integration', Chapter 6 in Peters, R. S. (ed.) *The Philosophy of Education.* London, Oxford Univ. Press, 1973, and also Hirst, P. H. *Knowledge and the Curriculum.* London, Routledge and Kegan Paul, 1974. Chapter 9 is on 'Curriculum integration'.

9 See Brunskill, R. W. *Illustrated Handbook of Vernacular Architecture.* London, Faber and Faber, 1971. Dr. Brunskill, who has acted as one of the Project's Consultants, has used architectural material substantially in work for children.

10 Some books written for children embody processes and ideas from the social disciplines with particular success. It will be appreciated that the use of such material by teachers as a means of building up their own understanding of the social disciplines is a quite different matter from using it as a scheme of work for children. There could however be some overlap between the two if teachers, having worked through the planning procedures suggested in Part 2, decide that these particular books do have specific value for their purposes with children.

11 A certain amount of light has been thrown on this question by studies of the impact on schools of curriculum development projects intended to promote integration. See for example Shipman, Marten, with Bolam, D. and Jenkins, D. *Inside a Curriculum Project.* London, Methuen, 1974, especially chapter 6.

12 Lawton, D., Campbell, J. and Burkitt, Valerie, *op. cit.* especially chapter 7.

1.4 The contribution of geography

Few disciplines have changed more in recent years than Geography, so much so that a veritable generation gap has appeared even among academic geographers; and increasingly among teachers too. So it will be useful first to indicate something about those changes, which are not familiar to everybody, and how they relate to the school subject geography, before considering the specific ways in which Geography as a resource can contribute to the middle years of schooling.

Geography as it used to be
Two generations ago, geography for the years between 8 and 13 still consisted substantially of descriptive, factual material, enlivened by anecdotes and examples, but explained in over-simplified terms and often associated with rote learning. Even one generation ago, it was quite usual to find geography beginning with tales of children in other lands, then touching upon the locality and the homeland, and embarking before the age of thirteen on a world tour of regional study. During those middle years there was some attempt to build up skills, especially mapwork, and concepts, but a great deal of the work was based on unique and colourful instances, interesting in themselves but not always chosen for their suitability as a basis for the extension of ideas. This kind of geography was relatively divorced from children's own experiences, producing somewhat opaque images of other peoples and cultures, though it did include, through local studies, something more immediate which was often taught in a lively and enterprising way. Even in local studies, however, opportunities for the systematic extension and enrichment of children's experience were often missed.

School geography of this kind was related to Geography as an academic discipline which was a deliberate combination of the physical sciences with other social disciplines such as History and Economics, and which laid great emphasis on the factors which gave regions their unique character. It was the human aspect of this Geography which predominated in school geography.

The 'new' geography
Changes in academic Geography itself have altered the character of the discipline, and these in turn are beginning to exercise a considerable influence within some schools. The main distinctive change has been to incorporate, as basic features of geographical study, methods which have hitherto been more typical of the Social Sciences, as ways of trying to explain and to predict what happens in particular locations. This goes considerably beyond the older lists of factors and distributions and makes greater claims to precision.

42

More recently still, close links have been made with disciplines such as Psychology and the other Social Sciences through a common interest in themes such as poverty, the developing world and the urban crisis. This does not mean that the distinctiveness of the contribution of Geography has been called into question, for Geography is still the discipline primarily concerned with location issues such as where people are, where they work, where they move, and how the flow of traffic and information and consumer goods are related to one another. Maps and their adaptations are still the basic means of conveying the importance of location and movement on the earth's surface[1].

One consequence of these new features in Geography is that more emphasis is laid on the methodology of the Social Sciences and on mathematical and statistical methods than was previously the case. This has brought Geography closer in nature to the Social Sciences, and indeed some people would claim that Geography should now be classified unequivocally as a Social Science, in a way that could hardly be true of History. Others would point out that this new status as a Social Science could carry with it a danger that these newer emphases might, instead of illuminating more adequately the human situation in Place as Geography is expected to do, lead to a retreat into statistical impersonality. To recognise this danger is to go some way towards avoiding it.

Writers about the teaching of geography at all levels are becoming increasingly aware that the distinctive features of the 'new' geography are matters which children can begin to appreciate to some extent in the middle years of schooling[2]. It is, for example, possible to apply simple models to problems of traffic flow and population distribution with children. An example of the first was carried out during the Project's experimental programme in schools, while the published unit on *Points, patterns and movement: detective work in geography* indicates how children can be helped to understand ideas of this kind. In fact, if Geography in its modern form is looked upon as a subject resource, then it has a great deal to offer along with other disciplines in respect of skills, techniques and insights.

Relevance   Firstly, it is relevant to children as they are now.
Teachers, perhaps unduly deterred by assumptions about
children's thinking misinterpreted from Piaget, have tended
to underestimate what young children are capable of understanding. For example, they have sometimes thought that
children were eager to absorb stories or descriptions about
other people, but were unable to investigate relationships
among other people or to interpret these in terms of their
own experiences. (See section 1.3 above.) The Project Team
found in schools that children could go much further down
this road than had sometimes been realised, and if this is so,
then Geography offers an inexhaustible source of situations
for comparison and contrast and for the fuller understanding
of their own situation, especially through the use of key
concepts as outlined in section 2.2. Here again, in fact, the
environment in the broadest sense is both content and
context of education.

But there is another kind of relevance too that can and
should emerge, one which is close to the Project's own values.
Geography studies people as individuals as well as their
relationship to a wider society. Just as geographers vary in
their interpretations, and just as geography teachers vary in
their methods, so they can convey through their teaching
that children, too, may vary in their approaches. Indeed, in
their attempts to order and organise the spatial aspects of
time and society, geographers, like the rest of us, are looking
through personal lenses, filtering new experiences of reality
through accumulated experience and custom to create their
own world view.

Moreover, although the eight- or ten-year-old's view and
interpretation will be different from that of the mature adult,
for the child himself it is his valid perception of the spatial
world and his construction of reality as he sees it. This, not
somebody else's statements, forms the real basis on which a
more thoughtful and informed perception can eventually be
erected. Geography, as a resource discipline, shows how
such perceptions of the changing spatial world can be
organised and interpreted. In a parallel, though more
rudimentary, way, children's own perceptions can be

organised, and each child can build up his own set of perceptions, related to his own experiences, abilities and potential, and adapted to what he encounters in school.

Critical thinking   One of the Project's principal emphases is on the value of critical thinking (sections 1.2 and 2.1). Geography can assist this development, through children's active participation, whether it is through the isolation of problems for study or the collection and processing of data to solve problems[3]. Related to this there is a need for children to realise and try to analyse the importance of values, both their own and those held generally in society, and how their values affect what they do.

Critical thinking at this level is obviously demanding, but geography affords plenty of instances in which it can be exercised. Examples of people interacting with each other in different physical environments can raise questions about the taken-for-granted nature and assumptions of life in the home, the local environment and the homeland, and can lead to a progressive process of reasoning about the causes of such differences, as suggested in section 2.2. Games and simulations can assist this process in an enjoyable way[4], but should not be allowed to convey the impression that critical thinking is something that can be introduced occasionally into a scheme of work and then laid aside. As will be indicated later in the discussion of objectives (section 2.1) it must be a fundamental element in the programme.

The use of critical thinking as a means of challenging statements, assumptions, and habits of thought and belief can also help to avoid one possible danger already mentioned in the application of the 'new' geography in schools, namely that the statistical, quantitative emphasis which forms a part of the new approach might displace the readiness to ask more fundamental questions. Measurement, comparison and significance are important ideas but they should not be allowed to obscure questions about the quality of life. There is little point in knowing how railways radiate from Buenos Aires and how the other nearby cities are patterned, unless at some point the children's critical thinking penetrates to the point at which they also invoke empathy and ask themselves what it is like to live there.

45

There are other ways too in which geography can contribute even more specifically, though at a less significant level.

Readiness to think in terms of spatial distributions   By this is implied the capacity to see the interrelation of the distributions of different phenomena on the surface of the earth and to represent these on maps or their equivalent: this is included under what has been termed 'graphicacy'. Some people regard the mapping aspect of spatial competence as a rather trivial matter, but there is an important difference between the mere acquisition of mapwork skills and the use of maps as a means of formulating new hypotheses and ideas. Sociology and Political Science and other Social Sciences do also of course use maps peripherally, but Geography is the discipline which assigns central importance to skills and thinking of this kind and which achieves most by such means.

A global perspective   One other way in which Geography as a resource can contribute distinctively to the development of children in the middle years is through the building up of a concept of the world as a whole, and of its variations and its colour and interest. Moreover, it can provide a more complete totality of Place than History can afford for the flow of Time, or the Social Sciences for the logically different notion of Society. For 'the round world' is there, as a finite fact, with the globe as its image. The habit of thinking about the world as a whole may again seem a relatively trivial one, hardly worth specifying as a task for schools in an age when the media seem to convey it so adequately. However, it still remains true that a systematic experience of Geography as a resource, alongside History and the Social Sciences, can give a powerful stimulus to the development of a global perspective and to the interdependence not only of Man with Nature, but also of Man with Man.

Three main approaches to geography teaching
The next point is to consider how these uses of Geography in the middle years can be effectively organised. In looking at the place of geography in schools during those years, teachers are, in fact, dealing with the complex interaction of three main approaches to geography: through the world

46

society, through the child, and through the organised subject-content of geography itself. Figure 2 indicates in a very simple way how they are related to one another. Teachers, in their preparation of schemes of work or individual lessons involving geography, may find this triangle useful as a reminder that, over a period of time, each approach should receive due weight.

But they need not all be equally represented in each scheme of work. For example, one month's programme could be deliberately centred on one of these three approaches. A teacher might decide that a class of eight-year-olds would gain advantage by starting from a topic within their own experience and related to their own environment, one within which considerable play could be given to their group and individual interests. This example of the child-centred approach could overlap with a second phase in which an attempt is made to introduce some basic ideas in geography. In this second phase the children might decide, after discussion with the teacher, to focus on some problem of general human concern such as the geography of hunger, and in this way as pupils progress through the middle years and as their learning and experience develop, they will also incidentally, but necessarily, become more versed in the use of individual disciplines as resources of ideas and techniques, insights and perspectives, as well as of information. It is for individual teachers to decide how to phase the sequence and

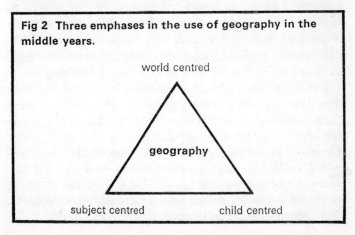

Fig 2 Three emphases in the use of geography in the middle years.

world centred

geography

subject centred   child centred

arrange the permutations, and further attention will be paid to these issues in section 2.4.

It is equally for the school to decide what aspects of the world scene to choose for study. Traditionally of course this concern has been dominated by world coverage, and most teachers are aware of the travesty of geography such an approach frequently produced. It is evident that the world concern in the context of the Project's work does not imply any ambition to 'do' Africa in a term, or the world in five years. It does however, indicate the obvious value of studying problems on a variety of scales, in moving the children's horizons from the local area to studies of other regions or other countries, planned in such a way as to ensure that different kinds of world context are adequately, and interestingly, sampled.

Focusing geography as a resource
For this purpose the teacher is faced with problems both of geographical element in distance and scale. As an aid to selection, he could visualise the teaching over the middle years being linked to some high definition camera orbiting the earth in a space capsule. He is at the controls. At times he will zoom in to give face-to-face close ups. In doing so he may have selected a culture group or area for detailed analysis. It may be a farming family in Honshu, a boy living in the suburbs of metropolitan Los Angeles, or a commune building a bicycle factory in Manchuria. In doing this, he will no doubt hope to capture much of the reality of life at a personal level and record experiences with which the children can readily identify either because they are similar to their own or because their difference is so striking.

But it will always be on a scale that is life-size and their own. It will be a type of study that may explore other people's feelings as much as their actions, and in the hands of sensitive teachers it can be used to paint an evocative yet accurate picture of life in other places. It will constantly relate back to the children's own experiences, environments and lifestyles, for on the basis of comparison the teacher will hope to throw shafts of understanding on what may appear at first sight unfamiliar and remote.

48

At other times this orbiting camera may be fitted with a wide angle lens to study bigger areas or aggregates of people. Such a definition could be interchanged, with the close-up lens being introduced to show how the family relates to the wider society, how the village relates to the countryside or town, how people move from one to the other, either on daily business and shopping trips or as part of short and long term migration, and how what is happening in one country may affect the lives of people in another.

This expanding awareness of similarities and differences, of isolation and contact, of conflict and consensus, will be a gradual process, and at no stage in the middle years is it envisaged that there can be a complete understanding of these abstract concepts. But as has already been indicated, the geographer is concerned with a dynamic world. There must therefore be times when the camera is fitted with a movie mechanism so that children can begin to understand the processes involved.

In adopting this approach the teacher has to face problems such as how to relate the specific to the general, the near to the distant, the concrete to the abstract, the static to the changing. Unless the focus is right there is still the danger of perpetuating hazy images of the real world which was one of the characteristics of traditional geography. The danger of bias, simplification and stereotyping are equally great, and in order to highlight or re-create reality it is obvious that the teacher will have to resort to the use of more techniques than the visual. In doing so he will need to provide a wide variety of resources through which the children can gain access to distant places, peoples and events. But if the aim is to build a curriculum with a truly global view these are all challenges that have to be faced.

References

1 For a useful general introduction to 'the new geography', see Graves, N. (ed.) *New Movements in the Study and Teaching of Geography*. London, Temple Smith, 1972.

2 A number of important books and articles have been devoted to the implications of the new Geography for school

geography, and to how the newer approaches may be introduced in school. See in particular:

Morris, J. W. 'Geography for juniors'. *Trends in Education*, 28 October, 1972.

Graves, N. (ed.), *op. cit.*

Walford, R. (ed.) *New Directions in Geography Teaching.* London, Longmans, 1973.

Bale, J., Graves, N., and Walford, R. (eds.) *Perspectives in Geographical Education.* Edinburgh, Oliver and Boyd, 1974.

In addition, the Geographical Association has published two useful handbooks:

Pemberton, P. *Teaching Geography in Junior Schools*, 1959.

Graves, N. *Geography in Secondary Education*, 1971.

Among attempts to carry these ideas through into actual work with children, see in particular:

Cole, J. P. and Beynon, N. J. *New Ways in Geography: A Guide for Teachers.* Oxford, Basil Blackwell, 1969.

3 Interesting examples of problem-centred work can be found in:

Ward, C. and Fyson, A. *Streetwork: The Exploding School.* London, Routledge and Kegan Paul, 1973, and

Coggin, P. A. *The Birth of a Road.* London, Rupert Hart-Davis, 1974.

The second of these books relates the participation of some Wiltshire schools in a study of the impact of the building of the M4 motorway. The first is a more general indication of the sensitive nature of the issues that can be raised through environmental education. Both are relevant to the general approach advocated by the Project. A more general approach to local problem-centred work has been devised by the Liverpool Educational Priority Area Project and expounded in the writings of its Director. See for example:

Midwinter, Eric C. *Social Environment and the Urban School.* London, Ward Lock Educational, 1972.

4 A number of guides to games and simulations have been published. They are referred to in the Project's own publication on the subject:

Elliott, G., Sumner, Hazel M. and Waplington, A. *Games and simulations*, Glasgow and Bristol, Collins/E.S.L., 1975.

1.5 The contribution of history

There is an amusing part in *The History of Mr. Polly* in which H. G. Wells describes his hero's education –

'Mr. Polly went into the National School at six, and he left the private school at fourteen and by that time his mind was in much the same state that you would be in, dear reader, if you were operated upon for appendicitis by a well-meaning, boldly enterprising, but rather overworked and underpaid butcher boy, who was superseded towards the climax of the operation by a left handed clerk of high principles but intemperate habits – that is to say it was a thorough mess. The nice little curiosities and willingness of a child were in a jumbled and thwarted condition, hacked and cut about – the operators had left, so to speak, all their sponges and ligature in the mangled confusion . . . He thought of the present world no longer as a wonderland of experiences, but as geography and history, as the repeating of names that were hard to pronounce, and lists of products and populations and heights and lengths and as lists and dates and oh! and Boredom indescribable.'

A caricature of the subject-centred curriculum of seventy years ago? Perhaps, but its characterisation of history teaching as preoccupied with specific information, with chronology, with memorisation, and unrelated to the child's experiences finds a ready enough echo today; for example, in Mary Price's comment on history teaching 'There are the strongest reasons for supposing that in a great many schools it is excruciatingly, dangerously, dull and what is more, of little relevance to the pupils'[1].

There are teachers who despair of finding any remedy to this situation. After all, so the Jeremiad runs, history is concerned with time and young children lack a developed sense of historic time; history is largely about adults and young children cannot understand adult behaviour; history uses present day language to describe past events, and young children's understanding of language is limited to their present day experiences. The Jeremiad continues, history as a school subject has received its *coup de grâce* from recent studies which have been done on children's thinking in history. These have shown, in broad terms, that most children aged between 8 and 13 can only think logically about what is within their experience, or what is immediately before them. They are unable to cope with the abstractions that the language of history employs, or hypotheses involving them: the very kinds of operations which a study of history seems to demand. So some teachers conclude that history is not fit for their pupils, and some scholars, that children are not fit for history.

In fact the real conclusion to be drawn from all this is not that we are wasting our time trying to teach history to young children, but that we are wasting our time trying to teach mature 'academic' History to young children by cutting out this and that, simplifying here and there, and trying, by whatever ingenious methods, to make the scholastic cap and gown into a schoolboy's jacket and trousers. We can only plan historical experiences and activities which are meaningful to young children if we go back to thinking what, fundamentally, history is about; plain cooking not *Cordon Bleu*[2].

The real significance of the recent studies of children's thinking in history is that at last we are beginning to accumulate some data other than classroom folklore on which we can base these teaching and learning strategies[3].

What, then, is school history about, and what opportunities does it offer to teachers who are working with young children?

Roots
Firstly, it is misleading to assume that history has nothing to do with the present. This assumption seems to be implicit in those chronological syllabuses which reserve the present for the end of the course and yet never quite get there. The past does not stop conveniently a few years short of the present. Past and present are part of a continuous process and if children are going to be able to understand the world in which they live, they need to explore what might be called the living past and they need to be made aware of ways in

which the past has influenced the present. They need, in Robert Douch's words, 'to be involved in history, to see it not as a film which they simply watch, but as a continuing play in which they are the actors'[4].

This means relating the pupil to his own past and through his past to his family's past. It means exploring the immediate physical environment. It means looking at the social environment, at games, at customs and traditions. It involves asking questions like 'Where was your father born?' 'Why is your street called Village Street when you live in a city?' 'Why do we celebrate Christmas with yule logs and fir trees?'[5]

Now it does not follow from this that to be relevant all history must be recent history, or local history. There is every point in encouraging young children to investigate a period in the past, or a past society, to try to find out how the people lived and what ideas about life they had and how these compare with their own. These 'Then and Now' studies are usually popular with pupils because they involve a wealth of concrete detail. What needs to be realised, however, if studies like these are to do more than engage the pupils' interest for a time, is that it is not enough to concentrate on the 'Then' and leave the 'Now' to speak for itself. Comparisons and contrasts, similarities and differences need to be consciously pointed out and discussed. If this is done, then pupils will be led to ask questions about their own society and will be able to begin to put their own society, and themselves, in a wider context.

Change

Secondly, and anticipating the discussion of the Project's key concept of continuity/change (section 2.2) history is about change, and not about chronology as such, or periods, or reigns. Older people, educated in sterner times, often boast about the thoroughness of their history teaching. Many of them can recite the kings and queens of England from memory and even get them in the right order, but this feat has little enough to do with historical thinking. Nor need we despair because yet another pupil has put George III before William III in a history test. Despair sets in only when we realise that there are hundreds of children following the type of chronological syllabus best characterised as a quick 'streak' through the ages who see a kaleidoscope of kings, battles, inventions and buildings yet don't really understand that history is about change.

Chronology, reigns and periods, as John Fines has pointed out, form a useful indexing system for historians[6]. We are in danger of studying the index and ignoring the book. The basis of historic time is change, and change is not only the essence of History, it is also happening all the time to children, and that is why history is relevant to them. With very young children there is something to be said for presenting past life in a static form, for example, the Victorian house, Victorian transport, Victorian costume. Older children however, ought to be given opportunities to do detailed studies in terms of changes, trying to find out what changes occurred during Victoria's reign, trying to assess how rapidly the changes occurred and trying to find out some reasons why these changes occurred.

In a similar way, there are a lot of 'traditional' topics which take on new meaning if they are looked upon in the light of the concept of change. For example, it might be hard to justify the teaching of eighteenth century enclosures to a predominantly urban population, but seen as a case study of change, how changes in agricultural technology and organisation, among other things, affected people's lives, it does become relevant, particularly when it can be compared with changes which are affecting people's lives today.

Enquiry

Thirdly, history is about enquiry. We will never know exactly what happened in the past. Our knowledge of the past depends on evidence which is usually incomplete and often conflicting. Even so-called historical facts depend on value judgement. As E. H. Carr puts it:

'The facts speak only when the historian calls on them; it is he who decides to which facts to give the floor, and in what order or context'[7].

If history is going to come alive and children are going to be involved in it we need to see it and teach it, not as a cut and

54

dried product, but as a process of enquiry. In Edwin Fenton's succinct resumé, we need to give pupils data to explain as well as explanations of data. So we need to familiarise pupils with the different types of evidence, and their limitations, to give them learning experiences which will enable them to evaluate evidence, to appreciate bias and conflict in evidence and to be able to draw conclusions from evidence. A programme like this may seem ambitious for 8-13 year olds, but it is important to begin laying the foundations early. In fact, much would depend on the type of evidence and how it was used. For example, young children would be able to draw some conclusions about what their area was like in the past by looking at street names and street furniture. Older children would be able to look at the evidence from the 1871 census enumerators' returns and mark out who lived in their area in 1871, what kind of work they did and where they came from.

In this way, through the study of history, children can begin to develop critical thinking skills and the ability to make reasoned judgements, qualities essential for a citizen in a democracy like ours. Because situations and issues in history are similar to those in everyday life conditions for 'transferring' these skills are favourable[8].

People

Finally, and above all, history is about people. This seems obvious enough, but it needs emphasising. Studies of the development of the steam engine, for example, which ignore inventors as people and the human consequences of the development are not history, but a kind of technological antiquarianism. History is about people, not people as categories but individual people, real people who lived, faced problems similar to ours, were successes or failures, the famous, the infamous and the obscure. Children learn about people, and form their own behaviour patterns, from parents, friends, peer groups, even the 'cult' figures that one hears so much about today, but direct experience of this kind is, however, necessarily limited. History offers an extension of this, a chance to examine and reflect on the motives, feelings and behaviour of a wide variety of people who lived in a wide variety of situations. So children need to be involved in what has been called the 'pageant' of history, its colour, its excitement, its drama, its characters through story-telling, a sadly neglected art in today's classrooms, through drama[9], through historical fiction and through role playing games and simulations.

By developing the young child's imagination in this way we can enlarge his vision, and by grappling to understand other people's behaviour, he can come close to understanding his own. Of course, if this imagination is to transcend the limits of mere undisciplined fantasy-spinning, it needs to be rooted in historical reality. Historical imagination is not opposed to, or even preparatory to the study of evidence which was discussed earlier. In fact historical imagination and critical thinking reinforce one another. An example of this occurring in practice can be seen in the work done on family history in which children use original sources and enter imaginatively into the lives of their ancestors[10].

Any attempts to develop an understanding of human beings and their relationships must involve an examination of the values which motivate human behaviour. Ask a child to imagine that he is a sailor on board the *Golden Hind*, and some discussion and understanding of religious differences and national pride become necessary. Not only does this involve difficult concepts, but it involves entry into an area of controversy, an area about which history teachers are particularly sensitive. For history teaching has been used in the past, and is still being used, to inculcate certain specific values whether they involve the glory of the British Empire, or the belief in America as the bulwark of democracy, or the cultivation of the Marxist-Leninist world outlook. The dilemma is in a sense inescapable. No teacher can hide his values. History, as we have seen, cannot be objectively written, but only with impartiality in mind. Perhaps this is the important distinction. Through imaginative experience in history young children can be gradually brought to an understanding that there are, and have always been, a wide range of differing values, and to some appreciation of the way in which values can affect choice of action. This is all the more important with young children because what

evidence there is points to the early development of stereotypes.

The essence of the matter

We hear a lot nowadays about Jerome Bruner's idea that
teachers ought to concern themselves with teaching the
structure of a discipline rather than its finished product.
This has prompted a great deal of activity on the part of
scholars and teachers. The results as far as history are
concerned seem meagre. Some have seen structure as the
historian's method, elevated in extreme cases to a six-point
mode of enquiry to which few historians would subscribe[11].
Others have turned desperately to lists of generalisations
like, 'Human societies have undergone and are undergoing
continual though perhaps gradual changes in response to
various forces'[12], which seem as banal as they are wide
ranging.

The assumption is rapidly gaining ground that if a discipline lacks an obvious structure then it lacks relevance. So, in
the search for this 'patent of nobility', history teachers are
very conscious of the fact that their claims resemble those of
Oscar Wilde's Ernest, who was found in a cloakroom.
But what makes a subject relevant is not structure so
much as what are its central concerns, and what, above all,
enables history to make a valuable contribution to the
development of young children is that human beings and
their activities are its central concerns.

References

1 Price, M. 'History in danger'. *History*, 1, 3, No. 179,
1968, p. 342.
See also Booth, M. B. *History Betrayed*. London, Longmans,
1968.

2 See the discussion of 'pure' and 'applied' history in
Watts, D. G. *The Learning of History*. Routledge and Kegan
Paul, 1973, p. 61 ff.

3 Recent research studies and the possibilities they present
are discussed by Thompson, D. 'Some psychological aspects

of history teaching'. Burston, W. H. and Green, C. W. *Handbook for History Teachers* (2nd edition). London, Methuen, 1972.

4 Douch, Robert, 'Local history' in Ballard, Martin (ed.) *New Movements in the Study and Teaching of History*. London, Temple Smith, 1970, p. 105.

5 On family history see Steel, D. J. and Taylor, L. *Family History in Schools*. London and Chichester, Phillimore, 1973.

6 Fines, John, 'Is there no respect of place, persons, nor time in you?' *Education for Teaching*, No. 86, 1971, pp. 52-57.

7 Carr, E. H. *What is History?* G. M. Trevelyan Lectures. London, Macmillan, 1961.

8 Some interesting examples are given by Edwards, A. D. 'Source material in the classroom', in *Handbook for History Teachers*. London, Methuen, 1972.

9 Fines, John and Verrier, Roy, *The Drama of History*. Clive Bingley, 1974.

10 Murphy, B. J. 'History through the family, 1.' in *Teaching History*, Vol. II, No. 5, p. 1-8. 1971.
See also Lamont, W. (edit.) *The Realities of History Teaching*. Chatto and Windus, 1972, especially chapters by Pat Kendall and Chris Crispin and note 5 above.

11 Good, J. M., Farley, J. U., Fenton, E. 'Developing inquiry skills with an experimental social studies curriculum' in *Journal of Educational Research*, Vol. 63, No. 1, 1969.

12 Jarolimek, John, *Social Studies in Elementary Education*. London, Macmillan, 1967.

1.6 The contribution of the social sciences

It is now several years since the Schools Council produced *Working Paper 39* - 'Social Studies 8-13', sometimes known as the Lawton Report[1]. This report provided the base line for the present Project, particularly with regard to the introduction of the Social Sciences as a curriculum resource for younger pupils. Its brief had been to find 'good practice' in the teaching of social studies and to consider the feasibility of introducing the middle school age group to the Social Sciences. The Lawton team were impressed by the scattered examples of social-science teaching which they saw, and recommended that such opportunities should be more widely available to pupils. This Project took up the challenge.

The nature of social science
The first, the central and the continuing problem was to communicate something of the nature of Social Science. A solution to this problem was made no easier by the range of social-science disciplines, Economics, Sociology, Anthropology etc., and the diverse perspectives within each of the Social Sciences, for social scientists are by no means agreed as to the questions which should be central to their enquiries. This was an important difficulty because it was essential for the teachers to understand that Social Science is a way of looking at the social world, rather than a body of knowledge about it. It is also the way of looking and asking questions which the Project Team has stressed as the central feature of the work to be done with pupils. For the Social Sciences are not cut and dried subjects which should be passed on to pupils. They are processes of enquiry, shaped by their times, the excitement of which pupils should share.

The first confusions to be cleared up in working with teachers were those already touched upon in section 1.3 about distinctions between social studies, social education and Social Science. It was stressed that social studies is the more inclusive term in that it can embrace several modes of enquiry, historical and geographical, for example, as well as the social-scientific. Social education, as usually understood, can be informed by these modes of enquiry, but it does not usually aim to produce the enquiring frame of mind which is the hallmark of an effective social-science education. Its aim rather is to help pupils to become well adjusted members of their own society. Unless a social-scientific element is included in social education, there is little hope of developing pupils' understanding of Man in Society.

This lack of clarity about the distinction between social education and social-science education merged with another confusion. Many teachers tended to interpret Social Science as the study of contemporary social problems. This is very understandable in that the mass media often present Social Science in the context of discussions on social issues. However, this is not, in any narrow sense, the central focus of social scientists, any more than the history of contemporary social issues is the central focus in the pursuit of historical understanding.

Pupils today are faced with rapid social change, and through the media, immigration and travel they are confronted by social diversity. All around they see signs that mastery of the physical world has not been matched by control over social changes and their consequences. At the societal level and at the individual level, the need to understand social processes is blatantly obvious. From the Project's experimental programme in schools it seems possible to say that pupils of the 8-13 age group find such an attempt interesting, socially relevant and personally rewarding.

The Social Sciences hold out the promise of understanding Man in Society; in particular of seeing the linkages between personal biography and social history. For as C. W. Mills has reminded us, 'Neither the life of an individual nor the history of a society can be understood without understanding both'[2]. He goes on to write eloquently of the benefits, and risks, of what he terms 'the sociological imagination', which he describes as the quality of mind which helps people 'to use information and to develop reason in order to achieve lucid summations of what is going on in the world and of what may be happening to themselves'.

The 'sociological imagination' involves the ability to consider the special qualities possessed by individuals, groups and societies and to trace the links between these different levels. It is a form of selfconsciousness, and through its widening of perspective gives the individual a new understanding of his life as it is located at a unique place in time and society.

In fact, another writer has defined sociology as 'the science of human freedom and of all the obstacles which this freedom encounters and overcomes in part'[3].

It is not an easy task to describe briefly a set of disciplines as diverse as the Social Sciences. However, they are held together by an assumption that man's social behaviour is not fully explicable unless the social context in which it takes place is taken into account. This may sound rather an obvious point until we remember, for example, that various attempts have been made to explain behaviour in terms of the inherent qualities of human nature. The list set out below attempts to give an overall view of the similarities and differences which exist beneath the umbrella of the basic assumption mentioned.

The basic substantive ideas of the social sciences
1 That men behave as they do because of constraints deriving from their social environment.
    Interrelated sources of constraints:
    a As they operated on men in the past.
    b As they operate on men in face to face groups.
    c As they operate on the groups and the subcultures of which men are members, by reason of the structural position of these groups and subcultures in society.
2 That men behave as they do because they respond to a social reality of their own creation.
    Interrelated aspects of the social construction of social reality:
    a Men perceive and give meaning to social phenomena and act according to the meaning they bestow.
    b They create new social forms and change the interpretation and evaluation of old forms.
    c They are unequal in their power to create new forms and meanings that will be accepted by others.
    Social scientists are divided in the relative weight they wish to give to these two sets of ideas, and this division tends to coincide with the extent to which they feel that the methods of the physical sciences are appropriate to the study of man in society[4]. Those stressing the first set tend to believe that methods of enquiry ultimately resting on the idea of control of interacting elements through experimental procedures are appropriate, with suitable adjustments. Other social scientists stress the need to interpret social behaviour through the exercise of empathy. Further understanding of

some of these basic questions can be derived from the study of some introductory sociological texts[5]. Examples could equally well be drawn from the other Social Sciences, though this is less immediately apparent from the texts at present readily available for pupils and young students. Whatever basic approach they adopt, social scientists try to go beyond the understanding that the active participant in society can achieve for himself, for he is normally limited by the range of his own personal social experience.

Social science in schools: the Project's approach
In so far as teachers wish children to learn to control their own lives and to contribute to the control of the social arrangements under which they live, rather than to be controlled by them, they will want the children to gain some acquaintance with the social sciences as school subjects. They can set about this in several ways.

First, the children can be introduced through a series of enquiries to a wider range of examples of social life than they would otherwise meet, and in this way an attempt can be made to extend their understanding of society beyond what they might otherwise achieve. This is not, however, a question of learning social science as a series of bodies of knowledge, but of using the Social Sciences as resources upon which to draw in order to increase understanding of the world. It is the process of enquiry, rather than the product of the enquiry, which is important.

In conjunction with this, children can learn to avail themselves of the social scientists' techniques of comparison and contrast. As will be seen in section 2.2 the Project places particular emphasis on readiness among children to perceive similarities and differences and to learn through comparisons.

At the other end of the spectrum, as it were, there is also the need for deep immersion in the unique characteristics of particular cultural groups. This is where the empathy objectives are so important, and discussion about empathy in sections 1.2 and 2.1 will make it clear that an act of empathy embodies cognitive and affective processes, as well as an act of self-control which seeks to refrain from judgement on the basis of one's own values. The empathy objectives are closely tied to the need for pupils to be weaned away from ethnocentricism, that is, measuring everything against the standards of their own society, in their evaluation of other ways of life.

In seeking to understand social life, social scientists also make use of concepts for organising their impressions. By means of concepts they try to group their impressions and to look for relationships among the groups of characteristics they have identified. These processes link in with the conceptual and other cognitive skill objectives emphasised by the Project (sections 2.1 and 2.2).

The concepts which the social scientists of different persuasions use are related to the questions they ask about society. This is no esoteric point because the concepts which we use are integral to the way in which we see social life and thus have fundamental personal and political significance. Therefore the concepts which children develop are of great consequence to them and to society.

This is a major reason why teachers should be on their guard against highly organised schemes for social-science teaching. Each such scheme is built around a particular conception of the nature of society. It allows the pupil little choice, at a fundamental level, between various alternatives. Most American schemes are like this, and though we owe much to American work in social-science education, this is something that teachers in this country would probably not wish to emulate.

The Project's approach in the light of the above points, has been to emphasise the development of the skill of conceptualising, rather than to prepare lists or networks of social-science concepts which might form the core of social-scientific work with pupils in the middle years of schooling. The topic-based approach results in loose ends and inconsistencies. This is just what is required, for the aim is to help the pupils to become more intellectually aware of the social aspects of their lives and to develop a curiosity about them. The Project Team do not think that an attempt to give a definite outline picture of the nature of society is either possible or morally defensible.

The Team do, however, think it desirable that certain attitudes should be encouraged, for without them work of a social-scientific nature cannot proceed in a satisfactory manner. Clearly the curiosity just mentioned is an essential pre-requisite to further learning. One way to develop this is to show pupils examples of ways of life very different from their own, e.g. Aboriginal culture or Inca society. The danger here is that these may be viewed as both exotic and inferior. This ethnocentric type of response can only be avoided if the pupils are given access to a breadth of information about the culture concerned; also if the teacher stresses similarities as well as differences between the other culture and our own, and if the teacher himself displays an empathetic attitude, not only in the lesson itself, but in any other classroom incident which involves a consideration of people who are different. For as Jackson[6] has emphasised for us, it is the 'hidden curriculum' which is so powerful in learning about matters of a social kind.

Other attitudes central to social-scientific enquiry are those of humility and scepticism. The first relates to our willingness to change a view in the face of evidence which seems to conflict with that view, or of an approach which seems to offer a more satisfactory level of understanding. The second relates to the necessity for the deeper probing of explanations which was implicit in the earlier discussion of the nature of social-scientific understanding.

In the face of all these requirements, dangers and differences of opinion one might be forgiven for asking if it is desirable that younger pupils should pursue social-scientific enquiry. The Project's answer is emphatically 'Yes'. Such study provokes reflection on issues which have always marked the minds of thinking human beings. To engage in social-scientific enquiry is to be released from the narrow boundaries of time, place and circumstance which confine us all to a greater or lesser degree.

Some practical considerations
If this is granted, there remain questions about how the social-scientific education of 8-13 year olds might be accomplished. The Team do not envisage mini-courses in

the various social sciences separately. Rather, they favour the topic-based approach, previously mentioned, where the various Social Sciences, History and Geography, can be drawn upon in various combinations, to illuminate a particular theme. The thorny question of sequence is also dealt with in more detail in section 2.4, but here it will perhaps suffice to say that the process is seen primarily as one which takes the pupils from a rough and ready level of understanding to one characterised by a realisation of the complexity and variety of social arrangements and the need for care in drawing glib conclusions from our own experience alone or from superficial study of a small number of examples.

In constructing learning experiences teachers must of course be influenced by the findings of specialists in children's thinking. The Project Team have considered the extent of the implications of Piaget's work for the social subjects. In this respect they owe much to the guidance of Professor McNaughton[7] whose work confirms them in their belief that the inductive method, by which pupils are encouraged to draw their own conclusions from specimens of data, is probably the most suitable for general use. It takes into account the 'concrete' level of thinking which tends to characterise the age group and provides opportunities for the development of the skills so central to social-scientific enquiry.

Mention ought perhaps to be made of the materials needed for social-science education. It is a mistake to assume that social-scientific analysis must wait upon the availability of materials about ways of life very different from our own, but there is no doubt that there is a shortage of well illustrated materials with texts at the appropriate reading level for younger pupils. Textbooks of pre-digested information are not the answer. Teachers look for sensitively written and carefully selected materials which convey the details of the fabric of everyday social life in other cultures. They need well illustrated resource materials about other ways of life, so that pupils can be stimulated to compare what they find in them with what they themselves experience. But the teachers, given time and opportunity, for example in workshops in Teachers' Centres, can do much for themselves.

Their aim should be a collection of raw materials, photographs, recorded interviews, newspaper articles, etc. which can be used as 'grist to the mill' of a multiplicity of social-scientific enquiries. The teachers with whom the Team worked appreciated these points, but practically all experienced considerable difficulty in respect of time, space and money.

A new emphasis

It will be seen that the work envisaged as appropriate in social science for 8-13 year olds, the work tried out by the Project in schools during the experimental phase, and which the Project has attempted to exemplify in its published learning units is substantially different from that which has characterised social studies for this age group so far. The history of social studies education[8] reveals a continuing concern to help the pupils to understand the social context of their lives, but the approaches developed in the past were those more useful for initiation of pupils into one particular society i.e. their own, than for engendering an understanding of social life. This latter does not result from studies of local services and detailed coverage of the 'facts' of the local environment. It requires that pupils should be given opportunities to compare their own society with those of others. In this way they can learn at one and the same time, what problems are common to men in societies everywhere and what is unique about the solutions achieved by men in their own particular society.

This type of study requires strenuous intellectual activity. It is not an easy option suitable only for the so-called less able. Nor is it appropriate only for those just about to be launched on to the labour market. It is an *education* which ought to be the right of every pupil in our schools. The evidence of the Lawton Report and the Project's own experiences in schools indicate that pupils in the middle years can both benefit from it and enjoy it.

References

1 Lawton, D., Campbell, R. J. and Burkitt, Valerie, *Social Studies 8-13*. Schools Council Working Paper No. 39. London, Evans/Methuen Educational, 1971.

2 Mills, C. Wright, *The Sociological Imagination*. London, Oxford University Press, 1959.

3 George Gurvitch's definition. See note, p. 124, in Filmer, P. *et al*. *New Directions in Sociological Theory*. London, Collier-Macmillan, 1972.

4 Dawe, A. 'The two sociologies'. *British Journal of Sociology* 21, 2, 1970, pp. 207-218.

5 For example Cotgrove, S. F. *The Science of Society: an Introduction to Sociology*, London, Allen and Unwin, 1967; Berger, P. *Invitation to Sociology*, Harmondsworth, Penguin, 1966; Riddell, D. S. and Coulson, M. A. *Approaching Sociology: a Critical Introduction*, London, Routledge and Kegan Paul, 1970.

6 Jackson, P. W. 'The students' world' in Silberman, M. L. (ed.) *The Experience of Schooling*. New York, Holt, Rinehart and Winston, 1971.

7 McNaughton, A. H. 'Piaget's theory and primary school social studies' *Educational Review*, 19, 1, November 1966, pp. 24-32.

8 See for example Rogers, V. R. *The Social Studies in English Education*. Heinemann, 1968.

Part 2 Some guidelines for curriculum planning

Part 2 is intended to make suggestions based on the Project's experience, to teachers who are planning curricula for themselves. Since most teachers will already be accustomed to some form of planning, the emphasis will be laid on the distinctive innovations which the Project recommends.

As with subjects, so again with the process of planning, it is necessary first to establish a terminology which will be used in the subsequent discussion. The first term to be defined is *unit*. This is quite a familiar term in curriculum development projects. In this case it means one relatively complete and distinct part of the work done by a class of children. For example, if a twelve-year-old class spends all the time available for the social subjects during four weeks on a study of water supply, then the organisation of that work, the materials collected or prepared for it, the time spent in carrying out, and the assessment made of the children's work, would be a unit. The teacher could characterise it afterwards, in his own mind, as a unit on water supply.

It will be helpful at this stage to make clear what the Project means by a *published unit*, since published units form a considerable part of the Project's list of publications. A published unit consists of materials for teachers and pupils, as well as information for teachers indicating how the particular published unit is related to the Project's recommendations set out in Part 2. It obviously differs from a complete unit, the sort that the Team and the teachers in the schools designed during the experimental phase, because the actual organisation and conduct and evaluation of the work, which then formed part of the unit, must in the case of published units be in the hands of the teachers who use them.

A third term whose usage in the Project must be defined is *theme*. This is straightforward. In the example just mentioned, the theme is water supply. A theme is therefore the actual subject-matter of a unit. When a theme has been chosen, a unit can be constructed on that theme. In order to assist this process, the Project has designed another publication, *Themes in outline*.

The choice of themes and the building of units is not in itself an innovation. Units of varying type and length figure widely in the teaching of the social subjects. They are sometimes designed for a class as a whole, but they may also take the form of group or individual assignments. It will be assumed that teachers using this book will be reasonably familiar with choosing themes and designing units of one sort or another, since this is the way in which the social subjects are widely taught.

It is also usual practice for teachers to consider the Project's 'four variables' - children, teacher, school and environment - to some extent in their choice of themes for units. They have to take into account what they themselves can do and like doing; what the children can do and like doing; what the physical resources and administrative arrangements in the school permit; and what other resources are available in the local environment. They also, especially in primary schools, regularly think about how the social subjects can be related to the rest of the curriculum and it is hardly necessary to add that the Project warmly agrees with all of these components of teachers' regular planning.

The one point that has been deliberately omitted from the discussion until now concerns the actual grounds on which themes are chosen. Why should water supply, or any theme, be selected rather than another? On what grounds should the social disciplines be used as resources for this particular purpose? The dictates of tradition, the claims of subjects for 'coverage', the requirements of future public examinations, the ready availability of materials and information, assumptions about children's interests, personal knowledge, preferences and beliefs, and even the very understandable tendency to repeat something that has proved successful in the past, all contribute to the actual choice of themes. It is here that the Project claims to offer something that goes beyond what teachers usually do, and to suggest instead something that the teachers working with the Project Team have shown that they can do, something that the Project's publications also exemplify.

The essence of these suggestions is indicated in sections 2.1, 2.2 and 2.3. It involves thinking about aims, deriving objectives from those aims, using key concepts as a means of drawing upon subject disciplines as resources, and developing themes into units by procedures through which the objectives can be effectively pursued. Section 2.4 takes this thinking a step further by considering sequence, why and how one theme (and unit) should follow another. Section 2.5 is concerned with how the work of children can be assessed if they follow units designed in this way. Finally section 2.6 indicates briefly the varieties of response to the Project that teachers display.

It must be emphasised that these suggestions are not themselves the central feature of the Project's recommendations. Certainly they are offered as the outcome of considerable thought and experience, as guidelines to teachers who are in the process of developing their own thought and experience in curriculum planning. But that central feature is that teachers should think *deeply, systematically and reflectively* about themes and units and the whole of their task, that they should work together to evolve a more purposeful curriculum in the social subjects and that they should develop the materials needed to implement it in their unique situations.

2.1 Aims and objectives

The first of the aspects of teachers' thinking that requires particular attention is that of aims and objectives. If they are to be adequately considered, it is necessary to give them a more extended discussion than has been characteristic of earlier parts of this book. For teachers who are not already versed - as a growing number are - in the basic ideas about aims and objectives current in curriculum development nowadays, it may prove useful to study this section and the following one carefully and in conjunction with some of the important recent literature about the curriculum in general[1]. This may appear to give considerable prominence to 'theory' in education, but this is what theory is for. It is not an obstacle to practice, but a means of ensuring that practice is based on adequate grounds and is likely to lead to an effective and defensible outcome.

The Project is as anxious as anyone else to promote what has come to be known as 'good practice'[2], but remains convinced that *good* practice, as distinct from superficially successful practice, depends on an adequate theory. The Project Team are therefore unrepentant about including a theoretical element in this central section of the book.

The relation of objectives to aims and values
It has always been necessary for educators to think in terms of aims, and to select aims in accordance with their explicit or implicit values. There has of course been disagreement about what those values and aims ought to be, but not about the importance of having aims and values. Even when the question was raised by Richard Peters, 'Must an educator have an aim?'[3], the real point of the question was whether he should have a grandiloquent, all-embracing aim which involved moulding a child in some particular image, or whether he should rather, as in the case of the Project, be content to develop with children a set of 'principles of procedure' and a generally encouraging climate in which children can grow and develop. Peters did not of course mean that an educator should have no general idea of what he was there to do: his later writings make this clear.

In fairly recent years, there has developed an increasing dissatisfaction with the mere statement of aims. It is not that aims have come to be regarded as irrelevant, but that they have come to be regarded as imprecise and inadequate.

The outcome of this dissatisfaction with aims as an adequate guide to practice has led increasingly to the introduction of an intermediate step between aims and detailed practice, namely *objectives*. The way in which this term is used is that objectives are derived from, and are meant to contribute to aims, but that they are relatively precise and sufficiently limited to figure as a useful guide to detailed curriculum planning and also as a means of monitoring the effectiveness of that planning. To take an example from the social subjects, it would not be very helpful to a curriculum planner to work solely from the aim 'to equip children to live in a world of rapid social change', but it could be of considerable assistance to consider objectives derived from that aim and phrased thus: 'the ability to recognise changes that are taking place in the local environment' or 'a readiness to accept, and adapt to, changes in classroom organisation'.

Both of these objectives could help to suggest ways in which themes and units could be organised. The first might suggest the selection of a theme concerned with change in the local environment; that might even itself be the theme. The second objective could affect the choice of another theme but it might also influence the way in which a unit, on this or some other theme, is designed, because the introduction of a new way of working could itself encourage children to take, within the confines of the classroom and the curriculum, a step towards the acquisition of readiness in this kind of adaptive behaviour. What is more, it is possible to assess to some extent, and more in the first case than the second, how far children have attained these objectives. For it is usually easier to estimate intellectual development than other kinds of development in children.

The introduction of the use of objectives into British curriculum development is usually attributed in large measure to the influence of the well-known *Taxonomy of Educational Objectives* evolved in the United States by B. S. Bloom and his colleagues[4]. This taxonomy was originally designed in connection with an attempt to improve examinations, and this may have set limits to its scope at the outset. It has been subjected subsequently to a great deal of general and detailed criticism, which cannot be adequately discussed here, though certain of the major objections do require mention in order to explain the Project's own approach to objectives.

One objection is that the taxonomy mixes up two distinct ideas. The first of these ideas is that objectives can be classified in a logical system (a taxonomy) and the second is that they can be arranged in the order in which, on psychological grounds, children are likely to be able to work towards their attainment[5]. Closely connected with this objection is a second, to the effect that the actual organisation of the taxonomy, its 'domains' (cognitive, affective and psycho-motor) and its 'levels', is tentative and inadequate[6]. It should be added that the designers of the taxonomy did not intend it to be taken as a blueprint and that these criticisms are examples of the further thinking that they intended to stimulate. It should also be said that the taxonomy has been found useful in many instances and that one project, *Science 5/13*, has given it an important place in its own strategy, linking it incidentally with a Piagetian approach to children's stages in intellectual development which this Project felt unable to transfer fully into the social subjects.[7]

The third reservation that has been made about the taxonomy is of a rather different sort. It can be illustrated from the example of the children encountering change. The point was then made that it is easier to assess children's progress in intellectual terms than in others. To take this argument a step further even within the intellectual realm (the cognitive domain), it is easier to assess their progress in the more humdrum matters such as the acquisition of facts and simple skills than in what the Project Team term 'higher-level' intellectual skills. Thus there seems to be a tendency, criticised by Hogben[8] and others, for objective-based curricula to be very much concerned with objectives that can be readily exposed to assessment. For these the term 'specific behavioural objectives' has come into use. A specific behavioural objective for the theme of local social change might be:

'a knowledge of the number of buildings that have been pulled down within half a mile of the school during the past year'.

The beauty of this, from one point of view, is that there is a right answer that can be ticked in a pupil's book. The limitation is that it is so remote from the aim from which it is derived that it does not contribute usefully to the planning of a curriculum unless it is linked with other, more intangible, objectives which might impel children to consider why those particular buildings were pulled down, by whom, at

74

that time; and to these questions there is no neat answer. Yet they approach much more nearly the real issues in social change. It is for reasons such as these, together with their liability to trivialise and even de-humanise education, that specific behavioural objectives have earned a great deal of criticism.

A final objection to the use of the *Taxonomy* as a guide to curriculum planning has been advanced by Eisner[9] and developed further by Stenhouse[10] and Chanan[11]. This objection, usually associated with the teaching of literary or aesthetic material, is that for such purposes it is not appropriate that aims should be implemented through objectives at all. For the aims, here, are more concerned with children's response to stimulus and inspiration and experience than with the development of specific qualities that can be designated in advance. Nobody can presume to decide for children how they should respond to clay, or to *Hamlet*. They should be left to formulate, in the course of their experience, what objectives they themselves think important. Indeed, the teacher's aim might well be to encourage them to do just that, in which case any prescription of objectives would violate the aim itself.

This general discussion of objectives is necessary here because all of these points were considered by the Project Team when they first worked out the strategy used in the schools programme. It is now possible to indicate how that strategy was developed, and necessary to do so if the Project's thinking about objectives is to be of value to others.

The evolution of the Project's thinking about objectives
The Project Team began by noting the widespread acceptance of the use of objectives in curriculum planning and by considering how far they should adopt a similar approach. At quite an early stage they decided to follow the general content of the *Taxonomy* to some extent, but to modify it in the light of the criticisms already mentioned. Bearing in mind the general values outlined in section 1.2, they agreed on the need to include among their general aims the fostering of *critical thinking* and *empathy* mentioned in that section and the further aim of *autonomy*. The first two of these do,

incidentally, correspond to Peters' 'principles of procedure' more than to his 'grandiloquent' aims, while autonomy, though more fundamental, is a basic aim very much in line with the avoidance of a 'grandiloquent' or manipulative attitude on the part of educators. Then, having also reconsidered the content and procedures characteristic of the social subjects and the properties of the social disciplines as resources, the Team put forward a classification of objectives based on two main categories:

Intellectual, social, physical skills
Values, attitudes, interests.

In doing so, they used the term 'physical' instead of Bloom's 'psychomotor' and, instead of making this into a major category of objectives as in Bloom's third 'domain', placed it among the skills. In this same group they also added a kind of objective which did not figure at all in Bloom's classification, namely social skills. (Perhaps it is not surprising that a taxonomy devised by examiners omitted this consideration). The values, attitudes and interests resembled to some extent the affective domain of Bloom's classification, but these objectives were brought together on the basis of general experience rather than on any technical grounds. The full table, in its eventual modified form, is reproduced on page 85.

The actual objectives were specified in broader terms than Bloom's. This was largely because of the objections to specific behavioural objectives already outlined. They were also arranged in an order which in the case of the skills, appeared to show increasing complexity but whose order made no claim to the sort of logical or psychological justification that is associated with Bloom's classification. The Project did not, in fact, produce a taxonomy as such. As for the values, attitudes and interests, which were later grouped under the rather lame heading 'personal qualities', it soon became clear that any attempt to invoke logical or psychological justifications for their ordering in the table would be so specious as to be indefensible. They, even more than the skills, were a collection of separate though important outcomes which, the Team hoped, would be assisted by the Project.

76

In this way the Project's first list of objectives was drawn up, and after discussion with teachers it was used in the design of units in the experimental programme in schools. In its original shape it took account of the first three objections to the *Taxonomy*, for it laid no claim to logical or psychological adequacy, it departed from strict adherence to the Bloom domains and levels, and it avoided, by dint of its very scope, undue concentration on 'low-level' cognitive objectives that are open to easy attainment and assessment. It was to be used as a checklist from which particular objectives would be specified for individual units, though over a period of time they should all be represented.

But almost as soon as this original list was in use, the Team began to be dissatisfied with it. There then began the process of 'awkward thinking' that the Project has described more fully elsewhere[12]. First, it became clear that the fourth kind of objection to the *Taxonomy* had a relevance to the Project that had been rather overlooked. For it was not enough just to avoid specific behavioural objectives. It soon became evident that for certain kinds of work in the social subjects it was necessary to defer the specification of particular objectives at least until a unit was under way. For example, the tradition of child-centred education carried with it an implication that children's interests should be a starting-point for a theme, as well as figuring among its objectives, and that these interests will only disclose themselves fully under the stimulus of the work itself.

Thus in one primary school during the experimental programme it proved possible, in the course of one unit, to extend physical skills much more than had been expected because it so happened that the father of one of the boys launched the class on a film-making venture related to the chosen theme. On another occasion, the introduction of group work in a unit became an important feature of that unit and so the social skills came to be unusually stressed. In yet another school the children showed unexpected interest in, and understanding of, issues during the Reformation in such a way that it became possible to incorporate into that unit a greater component of the 'higher' intellectual skills than had originally been intended, while there were other instances when unexpected difficulties in comprehension made it necessary to pay less attention to these higher-level skills than had been expected.

In all these cases it would be reasonably accurate to say that the relevant objectives were not altogether specified for the units; to some extent they *emerged* in the course of the units. Although there still remains a big difference between this process and the kind of curriculum which Stenhouse envisages, based on controlled input (of materials) rather than predicted output (of objectives)[13], yet it does represent a distinct modification of the originally-intended procedure in which the objectives were to be specified for each unit and to be collectively pursued by ensuring that, over a series of units, they would all be adequately considered.

Alongside this first modification another began to claim acceptance. It became clear that objectives, whether specified or emergent, were not something that could be attained in a simple way. The curriculum is not like a golf course in which each child plays the first hole (though some take more strokes than others) and then goes on with that in the bag to complete the other seventeen. Any objectives that are inclusive enough to be worthwhile, any, that is, that are not specific behavioural objectives of the most limited kind which the Project eschews, are literally unattainable. Mapwork, for example, whose importance in geography was stressed in section 1.4, is a skill in which young children can make a start; older children can become fairly, perhaps strikingly, adept, but even a professional cartographer cannot attain perfection in mapwork. There is always a farther horizon beckoning a learner, however skilled he may be. Again, nobody can ever claim perfection in the formulation and testing of hypotheses, or the enrichment of his interests, or in the way he chooses to participate in society.

Hilda Taba once spoke of objectives as 'roads to travel'[14] and it is an attractive metaphor, one that the Project has often used, though it does not quite bring out the degree of effort and frustration or the moments of achievement that characterise the movement of an individual towards that farther horizon. Perhaps a better metaphor is that of mountains to climb, where every now and again there is a level stretch or a subsidiary summit that is reached in the course of the ascent. It is these intermediate levels and subsidiary summits that mark an individual's progress. (At this point the metaphor fails, since there are higher and higher slopes beckoning up to an infinite height, and since in any case each objective is a mountain and all of them are being climbed at once: nevertheless, the roads metaphor fails at the same point).

Consideration of the impossibility of attaining objectives perfectly, and also of the way in which objectives could emerge during the course of a unit, eventually turned the Team's attention towards the inadmissibility of stating any set of objectives with any degree of finality. Their 'awkward thinking' obliged them to realise that their own ideas were changing and would continue to change, that the teachers with whom they were working had contributed to this change; also that the teachers' own ideas about objectives would become different from their own and that they too would continue to change; finally that if they regarded the autonomy of children, as well as the autonomy of teachers, as an aim (section 1.2) then children, as well as teachers, should be encouraged to develop objectives for themselves. Of course, this last point is different from the others because nobody expects children to talk the language of objectives and curriculum development. But it is both possible and desirable that they should learn to think out reasons for what they propose to do. With the passage of time they should think out reasons which they, and not their teachers or the Project Team or anyone else, regard as progressively more adequate. Some element of 'divine discontent' is a healthy element in the process of growing up, and it could well be true that the most promising 'output', in Stenhouse's sense, from education in the social subjects in the middle years is the establishment of a habit of mind in which children are ready to challenge their own established patterns of thought and behaviour in order to think and behave more adequately[15].

The Project's objectives in detail
In order to assist teachers in their own planning, and in their own formulation of objectives, it may be helpful to

indicate rather more fully the implications of the Project's table of objectives, in the final form which was agreed for the duration of the Project itself. This is reproduced on page 85.

Skills

Intellectual skill 1 is about reference skills, the hunting out of information. Even this one has often been omitted in the past, when in the social subjects the information has been handed to children in textbooks or oral teacher-tell lessons or even in notes. It is some advance when class or school or public libraries, atlases and magazines, are used. But reference skills mean much more than just looking things up in these sources; they include also the use of audio-visual references and of the outdoor environment. The Project's published units make a special point of invoking and exercising and developing all of these skills. It may be helpful to emphasise that the Project would include here some of the basic terminology and notation of the social subjects such as longitude, century, B.C. generation, cost, valley.

Intellectual skill 2 refers to various kinds of communication and these also straddle different media, including writing, drawing and painting, construction, map-making, taping, and the formal and informal use of mime, drama, movement and music, these last few overlapping with physical skill 3. These too are matters in which there is always scope for improvement and extension and for the development of a growing sense of coherence and form in communication[16].

Intellectual skill 3 is about comprehension and it is scarcely necessary to say what variety of opportunity is afforded here in history, geography and social science, though teachers have not always either appreciated how far children can take intellectual skill 3 during the middle years, or made its development a sufficiently positive objective in their teaching.

Intellectual skill 4 begins to approach the 'higher-level' skills. The mere discovery, communication and interpretation of evidence is a rather humdrum business unless some element of judgement is exercised about it. The Project's experience shows that children in the middle years are quite capable of this. However, it requires careful planning because, as was emphasised in section 1.3, in the social subjects there are often no 'right' answers and the one way in which the immaturity of children's thinking places clear limits on the social subjects is the difficulty that they show in accepting and tolerating ambiguity and uncertainty in explanation. (See section 1.2.)

Intellectual skill 5 is more wide-ranging because it involves the capacity to bring together disparate kinds of information and to 'carry' them simultaneously. Like intellectual skill 4, this makes demands that have been regarded, wrongly, as beyond the powers of children aged 8–13. It all depends what kinds of information they are expected to bring and hold together and this, too, requires careful planning, with what is relatively straightforward material.

Intellectual skill 6 embodies the basic techniques of the social subjects, and indeed of the social disciplines themselves. It is here that skilful discussion with children is needed, both to urge them to put forward hypotheses in the knowledge that they will not be ridiculed or rebuked for doing so, and then to urge them to see whether their hypotheses are justified as possible explanations and how far it is possible to extend them into generalisations, drawing attention to exceptions which can challenge these and lead to something more adequate. For instance, a class in a school in Birmingham might light on the hypothesis that the lusher parts of the city are in the south and west because in earlier times the wealthier people bought houses where the prevailing winds blew away the smoke from the factories: a nice, if oversimplified, interaction between the various social subjects. The class might then discuss this idea, find that it seemed reasonable, and go on to apply it to other cities until they met Stoke-on-Trent and Newcastle-upon-Tyne. At that point they might need to reformulate their generalisation.

Of course, it is not true that each of these skills is always more difficult than the one before it. The comprehension of a Cup Final or Test Match report is much easier than the finding of information about a mediaeval manor. At the same time, some uses of the 'higher-level' skills do depend on reasonable competence in the others. It is, for example, no use getting children to communicate or evaluate information about the distribution of retailers' premises, still less to formulate hypotheses about why they are arranged in that way, if they are not quite clear what retailers are or what the information that they have collected signifies.

Social skill 1 This is something which can be directly taught and practised in the school and classroom as well as outside. It is both an objective in itself, and a valuable element in the organisation of units (section 2.3).

Social skill 2 This may well be less familiar. It overlaps with some of the intellectual skills but the emphasis is on the word *awareness*, and to a less extent on *significant*. What is meant is that children should come to realise that there are groups which matter both to them and to the society in which they live.

Social skill 3 takes their own role in relation to these groups a stage further. But here again it should be emphasised that there is considerable overlap between these skills. It could well be, for example, that a child can be aware of how his own parents relate to a church or a club or a political party in a neighbourhood before he begins to understand that a powerful group of industrialists or a large trade union is important to *him*.

Social skill 4 This one is worded very carefully. If the emergent autonomy of children is to be respected and promoted, and this is an aim of the Project, then teachers, like the Project Team, have a kind of ambiguity-tolerance that they have to carry. They might wish children to grow up as active members of their own political party; they might like them to be good churchmen or members of a Civic Trust or eager revolutionaries, biding their time. But all that they can legitimately do is to confront them with challenges which render them willing to face the choice of participation. If, having faced it, they decide not to participate, that is their rightful choice.

Social skill 5 is qualitatively different because it relates directly to one of the Project's aims, the encouragement of empathy. It is therefore not one that can be encouraged in isolation for it involves other objectives too, as will shortly be pointed out. But it does make clear that there must be active opportunities for exercising empathy, through role-playing and sociodrama[17] which can be excellent fun as well as a serious part of the programme.

Together, the social skills are a series of emphases which are to be encouraged within units. Occasionally they can be more than that; they can suggest themes, and they can be the basis for the planning of units, as the Project's publications indicate.

Physical skill 1 This may seem obvious, but it is a very valuable supporting skill and when applied to simple recording and transmission equipment, as well as to self-reliance through outdoor apparatus such as the box compass, it considerably enhances the possible range of activity.

Physical skill 2 links this with intellectual skills 1 and 2, but it is useful to specify it separately. An interesting instance of this was the use of an 8 mm ciné-camera in a study of local evidence of pollution by a city school.

Physical skill 3 This is of a rather different kind, being again linked with intellectual skill 2 but this time in a more 'aesthetic' sense. In the Project's experimental programme this was particularly well illustrated by a primary school which exemplified the human consequences of a natural disaster through the use of expressive movement.

Physical skill 4 again develops the previous one to a higher level of organisation.

Personal qualities: interests, attitudes and values
These objectives are rather different in nature. Each of them is self-contained and largely independent of the others, but all of them are considered important by the Project.

Personal quality 1 This is clearly linked to the 'higher-level' intellectual skills, but the emphasis in this case is on encouraging an attitude of curiosity rather than a competence in formulation of questions.

Personal quality 2 This too is linked to the intellectual skills but is again independent of them. However, it is clear that the sort of teaching which can help in the realistic formulation and testing of hypotheses and generalisations can also encourage children to adopt the constructively sceptical attitude embodied in personal quality 2.

Personal quality 3 Children are here challenged to relate their experiences in the social subjects to themselves, as they are in the social skills, and in the process to work out ideas of what is a *good* example of an industrial town, a *great* civilisation, or a *bad* way of organising a group. This is a delicate matter to plan, for in a sense nobody knows how children respond: it is a private matter. Nevertheless, an encouraging climate is likely to exercise some positive effect.

Personal quality 4 This embodies the attitudinal aspect of the general aim of autonomy, since it implies that no one set of values should be embraced on the assumption that it will be final. Many adults would find this difficult to do, and though children might well prove more adaptable in this respect than adults are, they might literally find it difficult to understand what is implied. Not of course that this, or any of the other objectives, is something which teachers would actually spell out to children; but in this case it might prove difficult to convey the notion at all. Nevertheless, as a guiding principle it should be in teachers' planning.

Personal quality 5 Interests are rather different in their significance from attitudes and values because they are both a starting-point, and an objective, in education. This does not mean that education should go round in a circle because the objective speaks of *worthwhile and developing* interests which can enrich a child. This is a rather unpredictable matter but it is one which lies within the grasp of all children, and some of them do in fact develop interests which are remarkable in view of the apparent limitations of their measured intelligence and attainment. As an objective, personal quality 5 involves planning in such a way that individuals or groups can pick up suggestions and develop them during a unit, perhaps thus working out emergent objectives for themselves.

Skills			Personal Qualities
Intellectual	Social	Physical	Interests, Attitudes, Values
1 The ability to find information from a variety of sources, in a variety of ways. 2 The ability to communicate findings through an appropriate medium. 3 The ability to interpret pictures, charts, graphs, maps, etc. 4 The ability to evaluate information. 5 The ability to organise information through concepts and generalisations. 6 The ability to formulate and test hypotheses and generalisations.	1 The ability to participate within small groups. 2 An awareness of significant groups within the community and the wider society. 3 A developing understanding of how individuals relate to such groups. 4 A willingness to consider participating constructively in the activities associated with these groups. 5 The ability to exercise empathy (i.e. the capacity to imagine accurately what it might be like to be someone else).	1 The ability to manipulate equipment. 2 The ability to manipulate equipment to find and communicate information. 3 The ability to explore the expressive powers of the human body to communicate ideas and feelings. 4 The ability to plan and execute expressive activities to communicate ideas and feelings.	1 The fostering of curiosity through the encouragement of questions. 2 The fostering of a wariness of overcommitment to one framework of explanation and the possible distortion of facts and the omission of evidence. 3 The fostering of a willingness to explore personal attitudes and values to relate these to other people's. 4 The encouraging of an openness to the possibility of change in attitudes and values. 5 The encouragement of worthwhile and developing interests in human affairs

All of these objectives are intended, as has already been indicated, to be jointly pursued, throughout the years 8–13. Moreover, the two aims of critical thinking and empathy, and the additional aim of autonomy, outlined in section 1.2 are themselves linked with specific clusters of objectives thus:

Critical thinking   Intellectual skills 4, 5, 6
                                      Social skill 2
                                        Personal qualities 1, 2
Empathy   Intellectual skills 5, 6
                                        Social skills 2, 3, 5
                                        Physical skills 3, 4
                                        Personal qualities 3, 5
Autonomy   Social skill 4
          (especially)   Personal qualities 2, 3, 4, 5

It will be noticed that some of the objectives, mainly the 'lower-level' ones, are not specified as contributing directly to these aims. Nevertheless they are essential to the pursuit of these aims, since without them the other objectives are impeded.

With a table of objectives such as this, it is possible not only to pursue general aims but also to plan some sequence for work between 8 and 13. For, whatever else may take place, there should be progress and development in these objectives. This point, which is developed further in section 2.4, suggests a sounder basis for planning across the middle years than can be derived from a random selection of themes or an attempt to 'cover' history, geography and social science as such.

Using objectives in planning

There are two principal ways in which a table of objectives such as this can be used in actual curriculum planning, and there is a place for both. The first is as a 'map', relating one objective to another and indicating the total task which lies before the children and teacher during these years and beyond. This 'map' function can be extended further if the objectives for the social subjects are set alongside another set devised for some other part or parts of the curriculum, such as *Science 5/13*[18], and the 'maps' are compared so that the place of each in the wider curricular world becomes clearer. The other function is more evident when the planning is well under way, for in this case the objectives table is used as a checklist to remind the planners of what they have already undertaken and to encourage them to restore and keep a balance among the objectives in what they have still to undertake[19].

The use of objectives as a map and a checklist is an essential part of a teacher's equipment in the choice of themes and the design of units. Objectives cannot usually in themselves suggest themes, though occasionally there may be a place for the deliberate and direct development of one of them such as intellectual skill 4 through fictitious material devised for the purpose[20]. More usually, the role of objectives is in the selection of material from the social subjects which is considered likely to promote them. For example, there is little argument in favour of using watered-down textbook material or mere chronological or topographical lists, or even descriptive material with little potential for the stimulation of intellectual or social skills or the development of personal qualities. Thus much of the in-filling characteristic of the more old-fashioned courses in history or geography would be excluded. The same could be true of some of the flaccid generalisations occasionally made about the social sciences, unless they give genuine opportunities for the development of the chosen objectives.

It is not only in the choice of themes but in the development of units based on those themes that the objectives should figure in planning. To take one instance; the readiness of a teacher to think about the importance of the physical skills, and social skill 1, as well as personal quality 5, can lead to the use of a range of different individual and group methods based on genuine and well-thought-out principles. One particular device, that of questioning in a probing and challenging way, is closely related to intellectual skills 5 and 6 and personal qualities 1 and 2, in fact to the aim of critical thinking itself. Section 2.3 considers this issue at some length; here it is necessary only to note that the map of objectives raises such issues, and the use of objectives as a checklist before, during and after planning gives some indication about their effective incorporation into planning.

So much for the consideration of objectives in general: but teachers will ask themselves how many objectives should be incorporated within any one theme or unit. Ideally, they all should, and it really is necessary to ask oneself, every single time, about the relevance of all of them. This does not mean that they will all be actually used, equally, every time. During the schools programme the Team and their fellow-workers in the schools usually found that three, or four, objectives were much more in evidence than the others in a particular unit. There was some variation in procedure here because some teachers preferred to select objectives for emphasis and then look for themes that would give scope for this, taking the 'four variables' into account, while others chose the themes first, in the light of the 'four variables', and then worked out which objectives would in these circumstances be given most prominence. Both procedures can be justified, provided that the 'checklist' use of the table of objectives is brought into play to ensure that, over a period of time and in the design of a sequence of units, no one set of objectives is unduly neglected.

Objectives, used in these ways, provide a common purpose and a common principle with which to plan curriculum in the social subjects which is nevertheless entirely compatible with the four variables themselves.

The use of objectives however, requires implementation through a further consideration of the content of the social subjects and the procedures actually used in teaching them. The next two sections consider these questions.

References
1 There is now a substantial literature on curriculum development. Within this, good examples of writing about aims and objectives can be found. For a simple introduction to the general process of curriculum planning with one particular set of assumptions, see Nicholls, Audrey and Nicholls, H. *Developing a Curriculum: A Practical Guide.* London, Allen and Unwin, 1972. For a valuable compendium of relevant material see Hooper, R. (ed.) *The Curriculum: Content, Design and Development.* Edinburgh, Oliver and Boyd, for the Open University, 1971, especially Part 2.

2 The Schools Council itself has sometimes favoured the collection of instances of good practice as a basis for encouraging general improvement. This does not necessarily indicate what is good or why it has been successful in practice.

3 Peters, Richard, 'Must an Educator have an Aim?'. *The Listener*, 5 June, 1958, pp. 931–933.

4 Bloom, B. S., Krathwohl, D. R. *et al.*, *Taxonomy of Educational Objectives*. 2 vols. London, Longmans, 1956 and 1964.

5 Sockett, Hugh, 'Bloom's Taxonomy: a philosophical critique (1)' *Cambridge Journal of Education* No. 1, 1971, pp. 16–25.

6 Pring, Richard, 'Bloom's Taxonomy: a philosophical critique (2)'. *Cambridge Journal of Education* No. 2, 1971, pp. 83–91. See also, for a further discussion of the inadequacy of the notion of 'levels' in the Taxonomy, Ormell, C. P. 'Bloom's taxonomy and the objectives of education'. *Educational Research* 17, 1, November 1974, pp. 3–18.

7 Ennever, L. F. and Harlen, Wynne, *With Objectives in Mind,* Schools Council *Science 5/13* Project. London, Macdonald Educational, 1969. Objectives are also discussed in terms of the Taxonomy in a number of other projects such as the Nuffield Science series.

8 Hogben, D. 'The behavioural objectives approach: some problems and some dangers'. *Journal of Curriculum Studies* 4, 1, May 1972, pp. 42–50.

9 Eisner, E. W. 'Educational objectives: help or hindrance?' *School Review*, 75, 1967, pp. 250–260. 'Instructional and expressive objectives: their formulation and use in curriculum research and planning'. *American Educational Research Association Monograph Series on Curriculum Evaluation*. Vol. 3, pp. 1–18. Chicago, Rand McNally, 1969.

10 Stenhouse, L. A. 'Some limitations of the use of objectives in curriculum research and planning'. *Paedagogica Europaea* 6, 1970–71, pp. 73–83.

11 Chanan, Gabriel, 'Objectives in the humanities' *Educational Research*, 16, 3, June 1974, pp. 198–205.

12 Blyth, W. A. L. 'One development project's awkward thinking about objectives'. *Journal of Curriculum Studies* 6, 2, November 1974, pp. 99–111. See also the same author's chapter in Taylor, P. H. and Walton, J. (eds.) *The Curriculum: Research, Innovation and Change*. London, Ward Lock Educational, 1973, pp. 40–51.

13 Stenhouse, L. A., *op. cit.*

14 Taba, H. *Curriculum Development: Theory and Practice*. New York, Harcourt Brace and World, 1962, p. 205.

15 Professor A. H. McNaughton, of the University of Auckland, N.Z., who in 1972 spent a term with the Project Team, influenced their thinking substantially on this particular point, stressing always the importance of presenting children with 'dissonant facts' which would challenge their incipient generalisations. See the discussion of intellectual skill 6.

16 One important aspect of this, related also to the personal-quality objectives, has been explored by the Schools Council Project on *Writing across the curriculum*, directed by Nancy Martin.

17 An interesting introduction to the use of role-playing in relation to the teaching of history can be found in Fines, John and Verrier, Ray, *The Drama of History*. London, Clive Bingley, 1974. See section 1.5, above.

18 Ennever, L. F. and Harlen, Wynne, *op. cit.*

19 The distinction between the use of objectives as map and as checklist was clarified for the Project Team by two of the Project Consultants, Dr. Jeanette Coltham, of Manchester University Department of Education and Dr. John Fines, of Bishop Otter College, Chichester, whose own contribution to the literature of objectives in the social subjects is noteworthy. See Coltham, Jeanette B. and Fines, John, *Educational Objectives for the Study of History*. Teaching of History Pamphlet No. 35., Historical Association, 1971.

20 Some of the material devised by the Project for the development of evidence in the study of history was of this character. See the published unit on *Clues, clues, clues: detective work in history.*

2.2 Implementing objectives: an approach to subjects through key concepts

From objectives to key concepts
The use of objectives suggests why the social subjects, or other subjects, should figure in a curriculum. Together with the four variables, objectives can indicate something of the range of material within the social subjects that might beneficially figure in the curriculum in any one particular school situation. However, objectives and the four variables together do not indicate positively which parts of the social subjects should be included. This is because they are not directly concerned with the content of the subjects themselves. At one time, some writers did regard the content of subjects as one of the categories of objective[1], but this became confusing and the Project's terminology, in which subjects are considered primarily as resources, derived from academic disciplines, does not allow them to figure as objectives in themselves.

Yet there are ways in which the content of the social subjects, however organised, has clearly influenced the formation of the Project's objectives. Particularly among the intellectual skills, but also elsewhere in the table, it is evident that these are not general objectives but objectives for the social subjects as such, and the examples given in section 2.1 to illustrate these objectives are taken from the Project's field.

One of the objectives in particular, intellectual skill 5, (concepts and generalisations) shows this explicitly. In the context of the Project this implies concepts in the social subjects, concepts derived from the social disciplines, with which information can be organised with a view to the making of hypotheses and generalisations as suggested in intellectual skills 5 and 6.

91

These concepts occupy, in fact, an influential position in the table as a whole. The finding of information and its communication and interpretation are also linked with the development of concepts but the actual choice of themes to take account of the social and physical skills and personal qualities, is to some extent dependent on the concepts selected for development.

Therefore it is important to consider what concepts these are. In turn, this raises the question of the nature of the social subjects themselves. It raises it in a way that is rather different from the usual approach which thinks of history or geography in terms of accumulated knowledge distributed over Time and Place, and the other social subjects as primarily dependent on a collection of facts. The emphasis is laid instead on the concepts that are essential to the social subjects.

The term 'concept' is here used, and will be used in the remainder of this book, in a non-technical sense and refers to ideas, notions, principles inherent in particular fields of study, rather than to the concepts whose formation and attainment are the particular concern of cognitive psychologists, or to the logical status of concepts in philosophical writings, though these considerations have obvious relevance to the development of concepts in the Project's sense too[2].

Some of the concepts in the social subjects are comparatively simple ones, belonging mainly to individual subjects, such as shops and castles, but others seem more complex: for example, market, exchange and urban growth. So they can be classified according to their apparent complexity and sophistication. But there is another classification that may prove useful, namely by the range of objectives with which they are likely to be associated. 'Estuary', for example, might serve to bring together a quantity of information about trade routes in relation to physical features, but most of this information would be of an intellectual nature only even though it might involve the higher-level thinking skills, whereas 'emigration' could also invoke social skills (including empathy) and personal qualities.

Thus some concepts are simpler than others, and some more useful than others for the development of objectives in general. It does not, of course, follow that the simpler concepts need to be the least fruitful for this purpose. 'Hunger' is straightforward enough, but a theme about Hunger can promote nearly all the objectives in the table.

All these examples are taken from the individual social subjects. But the Project, through its consideration of subjects as resources in interrelation, was impelled also to look for some common elements that would enable this interrelation to be developed without destroying the specific contributions of the separate disciplines. After further discussion among themselves, the Team selected seven common elements of this kind and following the terminology of Hilda Taba though using it in a slightly different way, named them *key concepts*[3]. These seven key concepts were regarded not only as embedded in the subject-matter of history, geography and social science but also as being in a special sense relevant to major social issues today and thus also important for social skill 2: 'an awareness of significant groups within the community and the wider society'.

The point about key concepts is not that they are logically basic to the social disciplines located through some exhaustive process of philosophical analysis, but that they are practically related to a whole series of other, more limited, concepts and can thus be used effectively in the selection and arrangement of material drawn from the social subjects.

Even so, they are not the sort of concepts that can be adequately grasped by young children generally, though even this is sometimes possible and as the years between 8 and 13 pass, some children at least will be able to use and begin to understand the actual terms. Their principal function is to

---

Footnote
To those who have worked with Bruner's *Man: A Course of Study*[4] the notion of key concepts may seem familiar. They are, surely, very like the three ideas around which the 'spiral curriculum' is built:

What is human about human beings?
How did they get that way?
How can they be made more so?

or Bruner's five distinguishing criteria of human society; tool-making, language, social organisation, education, and the urge for reflection and explanation.

Children, in Bruner's project, move all the time a little nearer to the attainment of these ideas although the actual means of doing is

enable *teachers* to see subject-matter from a new and more
co-ordinated standpoint and thus to plan, over the years, a
relatively coherent progression in concept-development,
without being bound to any specific historical, geographical
or social-science content.

The Project's list of key concepts
The original list of seven, which the Project Team preferred
to other possible claimants for inclusion, was:

Communication	
Power	meaning social power, not energy as such
Values and beliefs	these were taken together owing to their close relationship
Conflict/consensus	a 'bipolar' one, indicating opposite ends of a continuum
Similarity/difference	'bipolar' again
Continuity/change	yet another 'bipolar' one
Causality	this was later altered to Causes and Consequences

One of the first points that may occur to anyone thinking
about these is that they closely resemble the objectives. This
is because, not surprisingly, there is a correspondence
between what appears desirable in the education of children
and what appears significant about Man in Place, Time and
Society.

A closer look at the list of key concepts, however, brings
out an important distinction among them. As the Team came

---

related to their development and to the circumstances in which they
learn. But Bruner's strategy started from the notion of a common core
in the curriculum which, as indicated in the Introduction, this
Project rejected. Thus Bruner's materials as an approach to subjects
are central and the adaptation to circumstances follows, whereas in
this Project the circumstances and the process of teachers' thinking
about aims and objectives are central and the materials are intended
only as examples of possible approaches to subjects as resources
through key concepts provisionally selected. Teachers may like to
discuss, as part of their own thinking, whether or not M.A.C.O.S.
and this Project represent fundamentally different sets of values, or
whether they are different routes to a common goal.

to realise, they really include two kinds, which can be called *substantive* and *methodological* respectively. The last three are methodological, that is, they are concerned with ways of classifying and thinking about subject-matter. The first four, however, refer to the subject-matter itself. Communication does take place, Power is social reality, and so on, whereas Change is a way of classifying what happens in Communication and Power. Of course, this is not a hard-and-fast distinction, since an observer's own values and beliefs will affect what he chooses to notice, while some people find Conflict/consensus useful as a means of classification. However, the division between the four substantive and the three methodological key concepts does largely hold, and has been found practically useful during the Project's experimental programme.

Some teachers have found these seven key concepts themselves rather hard to grasp. It may be useful to illustrate them by giving some idea of their range of meaning. Taking the substantive ones first, their significance can be shown by giving some examples (not, of course, a complete list) of subordinate concepts which they bring together.

Key concept	Examples of subordinate concepts
Communication	language, movement, signal
Power	control, production, command
Values and beliefs	obedience, progress, nationalism
Conflict/consensus	agreement, rebellion, contract

These rather abstract subordinate concepts are themselves different in turn from the more definite specific concepts which usually figure in discussion of curriculum content such as: import, railway, tribe. There is an interesting relationship between these specific concepts and the key and subordinate concepts. For specific concepts are hardly ever themselves derived directly from key or subordinate concepts. Rather, they are illuminated and enriched by all of them. If we take 'uniform' or 'market', for example, it is possible to link both of these specific concepts to *all* the terms in the table: think for example how uniform relates to signal, obedience, rebellion, or market to contract, production, movement. Other specific concepts do perhaps relate more nearly to some key or subordinate concepts than do

95

others, as can be illustrated by looking at 'pipeline' or 'totem' or 'aircraft'.

The three methodological key concepts, being rather different, are better illustrated by categories within which they apply than by subordinate concepts.

Key concept	Examples of category
Similarity/difference	size, importance, organisation
Continuity/change	time, sequence, process
Causes and consequences	purpose, chance, concomitance

These categories can also illuminate specific concepts but in a rather different way. If we think again about the five examples just considered, that is: uniform, market, pipeline, totem and aircraft, it is possible to see what additional ways of looking at each of them are suggested by Similarity/difference, Continuity/change, and Causes and consequences, and their categories.

In practice, the relationship between the three methodological key concepts is itself quite important. For example, there is one sense in which Continuity/change is a special case of Similarity/difference, and it is clear from the Project's experience that Similarity/difference is of all the methodological key concepts the one that presents itself most immediately as a classificatory device, with Difference a little easier to convey than Similarity. (See section 2.4)

This key concept is however a device that must not be used in too crude, or too subtle, a way. Children do not need to have the unfamiliarity of jungle life, or the reality of social-class differences, spelled out to them, but they may find it hard to appreciate the significance of the similarities or the differences between, say, Havana and Caracas. In fact, Similarity/difference might be adjusted to the knowledge and sophistication of particular children with particular teachers in particular schools in particular environments, as with all the other aspects of the Project's strategy. Section 2.4 indicates, too, how Similarity/difference can figure in the planning of sequence. (See section 1.5)

Continuity/change itself is a little more intricate than appears at first. Just as Difference is at first easier to emphasise than Similarity, so Change is easier than Continuity. A simulation of a Parliament under Elizabeth I would attract more attention when compared with one under Elizabeth II through its obvious contrasts of speech, dress and manner than through its similarity of procedure. However, there can be a startling instigation of interest when a photograph of the local High Street in the 1890's shows, among the trams and carriages and voluminous clothing, the Town Hall and a row of shops almost as they appear today. This last point also brings out the importance of using Continuity/change to etch out the contours of the largely unnoticed present and to give it new significance, by means of 'Then/Now' contrasts.

It is however possible to explore the full possibilities of Continuity/change through 'Then/Then' contrasts. These are of two kinds. One is the contrast between two places at one time in the past, for example, between town and country in Chaucer's England, and this in itself requires some conceptual maturity. The other, the contrast between two past times in the same place, for example between the Liverpool of the slave traders and the Liverpool of the Irish immigration, is still more difficult. During its schools programme the Project Team tended to overestimate children's capacity to make this fine discrimination during the earlier part of the middle years. However, all these skills do develop over the period 8–13 and indicate a second way in which sequence can be planned.

The connection between both of these two methodological key concepts and the third, Causes and consequences, arises through the need to consider why some things differ from others, and why things change. Admittedly, this is philosophically treacherous ground, but children have to tread lightly across it if they are to make sense of their social world. In this case too there is a necessary scope for progression from the understanding of simple causation, such as the building of factories near a new road, to the much more difficult matter of looking at complex situations in which several causes and several consequences are involved. Or what can well be more difficult still, examining situations about which too little is positively known for any one explanation to be warranted. (See the discussion of intellectual skill 4 in section 2.1.) Historical study often reveals situations of this kind, simply because so little of the complete story has survived from the past, but to any one individual a modern problem with a geographical or social-science emphasis, such as population distribution or inflation, can be at least equally baffling. However, Piaget and his followers have given teachers a line to follow – as they have rarely done outside the mathematical-scientific area – since they have indicated that the deployment of hypothetical or 'propositional' thinking to solve complex social problems does not usually take place before adolescence. This, too, is a clue for the development of progression and sequence.

A word of warning may be in place here. The problem for teachers is not to find complex situations but to find simple ones. Most of those that initially appear simple, such as rural villages and pre-literate societies, turn out to be almost as complicated as urban societies. The search for simplicity in subject-matter must be deliberately undertaken with a view to choosing, from the complex whole, aspects such as the ways in which physical features relate to lines of communication, or people's life-styles to where they live.

It is evident that nobody can think or read much about the social subjects or more generally about Man in Place, Time and Society without some indication of one or more of these key concepts, subordinate concepts and categories, one or two of which might of course themselves be regarded as ranking for inclusion in the list of key concepts. It would indeed be quite possible to regard interdependence, or culture, as one of these, and perhaps to relegate to the status of subordinate concept or category one or more of the Project's list, provided that this process of promotion and relegation can be adequately justified. For, as has already been indicated, there is nothing sacrosanct about the original seven. They are not Seven Pillars of Wisdom; on the other hand, they have at least something in common with any similar list, produced by other people, that the Project Team has come across.

Using key concepts: an example
The Project Team has spent a considerable amount of time discussing the use of key concepts with teachers, both in the

school trials and in the diffusion phase. From this experience it appears that teachers use key concepts for the implementation of objectives, just as they use the objectives themselves, in two principal ways:

a in the selection of themes

b in the organisation of work in units when themes have been selected.

In the course of deciding about themes, a teacher comes to the point at which, say, two themes, the Peak District and Sheffield, both appeal to him as suitable for his own situation and starting-point and for the children, school and environment in whose case objectives are to be implemented. From the point of view of History, Geography and Social Science they both offer considerable potential. Now, a teacher planning without the aid of key concepts might next spin for each of these themes a 'topic web'. The outcome might be something like figure 3 or figure 4.

Many teachers are familiar with this way of proceeding, and obviously it can be effective, to a certain degree, in implementing the sort of objectives discussed in section 2.1. But in the process there is no guarantee that concepts will be developed in more than a haphazard fashion. The use of key concepts adds a powerful tool to the equipment which teachers have for choosing and developing themes with the systematic development of concepts clearly in mind. The next step would be to look at the two possible themes and to draw on the social disciplines as resources to yield specific concepts illuminated by the seven key concepts. See table 2.

Of course, this is how a teacher would think of the two themes, not the words or ideas that he would put directly to children. But it should give some indication of the additional process involved in using key concepts in the consideration of the social disciplines. This the Project describes as *screening*.

Having thought about the two themes, he would now have some idea of the ways in which they could be treated. It now becomes necessary to use key concepts in the two steps previously mentioned, namely the choice of the theme and the way it is to be implemented. The second step will

Fig 3

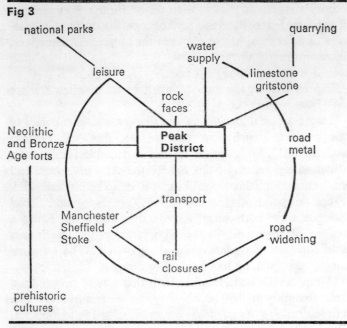

Fig 4

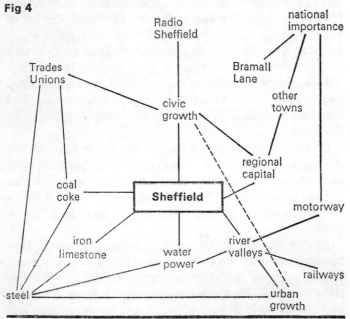

obviously affect the first; the choice of a theme depends largely on how it is to be tackled.

If we consider this second point first, it is now possible, in the light of the 'screening' already carried out, to look at the potential of each theme as it would appear if prominence were given to one of the key concepts rather than another. For example, Sheffield might be considered mainly according to Power, or the Peak District mainly according to Values

Table 2

Key Concept	Peak District	Sheffield
Communication	Routeways; materials; access to leisure pursuits	Routeways; regional centre; multicultural contact.
Power	Prehistoric forts: Duke of Devonshire; dependence on outside decision making	Exploitation of coal, coke and steel; social and political power.
Values and Beliefs	Survival of earlier value-systems; value of leisure pursuits.	Emergence of the social values of a modern city
Conflict/ Consensus	Conflict over the use of open country, and transport routes; consensus over local autonomy.	Conflict of interests in the main industries and occupations and local groups; degree of civic consensus.
Similarity/ Difference	Limestone and grit-stone country; similarity of institutions.	City and suburb; heavy industry and light industry; employer and employed; similarity of local patriotism.
Continuity/ Change	Continuity in hill farming; change in economic use (extraction, water supply) and in role as 'lung' for three cities.	Transformation from a rural area to a Victorian industrial city and again to a modern regional centre: continuity in buildings and institutions.
Causes and Consequences	Individual instances, related to a complex system (a rural area may appear deceptively simple).	A clearly inter-related complex: (a city looks as complex as it is).

and beliefs. It could well be that the teacher feels that in the general development of ideas in his class, a point has been reached at which one of the key concepts requires particular emphasis and that the potential for that concept of a particular theme (say, Sheffield in relation to Power) appears to make Sheffield especially suitable for his purpose. In that case, having chosen this particular way of treating Sheffield, and thus completing the second step, he is in a position to go back and take the first step by choosing Sheffield rather than the Peak.

It should by now be clear that key concepts can be a useful aid in assessing the potential of themes for the implementation of objectives. But it should also be clear that they are not automatic devices whereby a teacher can have decisions made for him. They are, instead, means of aiding him to think – in the words already used frequently in this book – deeply, systematically and reflectively about what he is doing. Consequently (and perhaps irritatingly at first) they do not give slot-machine answers. Indeed, two equally able and experienced teachers may illustrate the flexibility of the teacher variable by using them to evolve opposite answers, one choosing the Peak and the other Sheffield for equally good reasons, one perhaps treating his theme with an emphasis on Communication and another on Conflict/consensus. Similar considerations would apply to the choice between other possible pairs of themes such as:

The Coming of the Saxons
The Coming of the Vikings

A Chinese commune
Canadian lumberjacks

Victorian fashions
The Aztecs

Our Local Council
Adolescence

The value of considering these pairs is not, of course, to find which of the two is 'better', for children 8–13. Even though individual teachers may have quite strong views on one or more of these, they may well find others whose views are equally strong in the opposite quarter.

Using key concepts: some general considerations
Over a period of time, key concepts need also to be developed and made more explicit: this is one of the ways in which sequences can be planned (see section 2.4). At first, with the younger children, key concepts could only figure in the teacher's planning but before they reach the age of 13, some at least among the children can begin to use the key concepts and their names for themselves. As indicated in the conclusion (section 3.4), research into children's capacities to grasp key concepts, and into the order in which different children grasp them, is urgently required and it is unfortunate that this need could not be met in the course of the Project itself.

As teachers use key concepts in planning not only themes and units but also sequences, their own values are likely to become more clearly evident. The choice of substantive and methodological key concepts will reflect how teachers think society works and what developments they would like to see. There is a danger that this reflection of personal values might unduly distort the emphasis in the work which individual teachers plan for particular children. If this were to happen, the result would be unduly dogmatic. But the Project Team believes that a frank and responsible use of the table of objectives, together with an open-minded use of the disciplines as resources, constitutes an effective defence against such dogmatism among teachers who have genuinely given deep, systematic, and reflective thought to what they are doing.

In any case, it is necessary to remember that the promotion of autonomy for children is one of the Project's general aims and that a truly child-centred approach implies that children want and need to interpret their own social world in their own developing way, as Entwistle emphasises[5]. Thus a teacher committed to the Project's values should be restrained from dogmatism both by his respect for the subjects as disciplines and by his concern for the autonomy of children. (He is, of course, free to exercise his own autonomy within the teacher variable by rejecting this aim for his pupils, but in doing so he would depart in a fundamental way from the values in which the Project's strategy is grounded).

103

*Objectives, key concepts, subjects, themes and units: two
examples*
This section, and its predecessor, have been necessarily
concerned with a wide range of issues of a theoretical nature.
Although they are intended as a basis for practice, and
although they have been illustrated with specific examples
drawn from the Project's practical experience, they do not in
themselves state how the process of curriculum planning can
be conducted in detail. This is right. The Project's strategy
does not permit any dictation of this kind.

The published units do, especially through the Teachers'
Guides, show examples of how themes and units have been
worked out but it may be helpful, in addition, to conclude
this section with short summaries of the way in which two
different styles of unit, based on different sorts of theme,
could be devised by teachers starting to use objectives and
key concepts.

Example 1
With a nine year old class, the four variables as follows:
Children: mixed, a wide range of background and attainment
and experience of topic-based work by individuals and
groups, much of it in the social subjects.
Teacher: non-specialist, three years' experience, interested in
child-centred education and in social issues.
School: junior mixed[6], fairly formal in organisation but
allowing individual teachers considerable scope for initiative.
Environment: city, mainly working-class but with some
lower-middle-class families; mixture of council housing and
small owner-occupied properties; some local industries and
considerable traffic congestion.
This is the situation in which the teacher has to plan. Taking
account of the variables and of the issues that occur to him as
important in a study of Man in Place, Time and Society, he
provisionally suggests to himself Pollution as a possible
theme. Without the thinking suggested by the Project, he
might then spin a topic web as mentioned earlier in this
section and, after introducing the theme to the children,
work out with them some interesting ideas to follow up.
The difference made by using the Project's approach shows
in the next steps.

Objectives It is not just desirable, but essential, to ensure that a potential theme, and any unit constructed around it, should be capable of promoting a range of objectives. The teacher might well test Pollution against this touchstone and conclude that the main objectives that could be developed through this theme in his particular situation be:

Intellectual skills 3 and 4: interpreting and evaluating information

Social skill 1: small groups

Physical skill 2: using equipment

Personal quality 3: personal values

It is not implied that these are the only objectives involved, or that this is likely to be the set of objectives most prominent for every class undertaking work of this sort. Another nine-year-old class might, for example, be judged by its teacher to be more ready to develop Intellectual skill 5 (concepts and generalisations) than this teacher believes his class to be, at their present stage. Or, the work could be planned in such a way as to encourage those who are beginning to develop this skill to extend themselves further without rushing the others too precipitately into it: this point would have to be deferred until the planning of the unit itself is worked out. But one thing is fairly clear: the potentialities of Pollution as a theme are sufficient to warrant its retention, provided that it is sensitively and productively treated. (It might be difficult to justify the retention of many hoary themes from history and geography with as much confidence.)

Key concepts The next step would be to plan actual content and for this purpose it is necessary to look at Pollution again from one particular point of view within the general framework of objectives, namely its potentiality for the development of substantive and methodological key concepts. This, as has been indicated, depends to some extent on the teacher's own preference and emphases and it is likely that in this case his readiness to pursue the theme, and his policy in organising a unit around it, will be influenced by the social commitment that he as a person has. So he needs next to think about the possibilities of Pollution in relation to each of the seven, much in the same way as was indicated in the example of the Peak

District and Sheffield. It is reasonable to say that he will find some way of illuminating his proposed theme from any or all of them; it therefore passes, as it were, a second test of eligibility for choice as a theme. But he now has to decide which of the key concepts he will in fact use. His choice, initially, is for Conflict/consensus and Causes and consequences but, reflecting on the general pattern of development among the children and on the likely ways in which the disciplines as resources could be used, he decides after all that Values and beliefs, with Similarity/difference, would be a better choice, more suitable for the children's development but almost equally compatible with his own concerns. Having selected these key concepts he can also think of some specific concepts related to Pollution which can be illuminated by Values and beliefs and Similarity/difference, such as litter, fumes, responsibility, which can give further direction to his planning.

Subjects as resources   With these two key concepts he then has to 'screen' the academic disciplines as resources. Being a generally-trained teacher and not a specialist, he does not find this easy and has to consult others, including colleagues, a librarian, and other contacts he has made through the teachers' centre (see section 3.1). But since his concern is with Values and beliefs and with Similarity/difference, he finds that urban Geography and urban Sociology provide the best range of material. However, since he is becoming aware of the possibilities of using the social disciplines in an interrelated way, he will bear in mind how, for example, History and Psychology, and indeed some of the more accessible information about the significance of Pollution in Human Biology and Community Health, could be useful. Obviously he has to set limits to what he can read and find out by direct observation and otherwise, since one of the ways in which the teacher variable is important is that teachers do not overstretch themselves by setting themselves impossible tasks. (If they do, not only will they be less effective people as teachers but they will probably end by abandoning the task and reverting to their earlier practices. The Project does not aim to advance by expecting the impossible and achieving the negligible).

Planning the unit The final, and practically the most demanding, step, as any teacher knows, is to plan what actually to do. The use of objectives and key concepts and subjects as resources gives a firmer justification for the choice of a theme and a surer guide to what to do, but at this final stage in the planning of a particular unit objectives and key concepts can also influence the choice of procedures. For example, social skill 1 suggests an emphasis on group work. Physical skill 2 indicates the value of going out in this industrial and congested environment and collecting first-hand evidence by observation, sketching, taping, photographing, recording with the simple equipment used in field work etc: the interpretation of this is in turn related to intellectual skill 3 (interpreting information).

The decision about *what* to go out and find is related to the key concepts. For example, there could be contrasts between the quieter residential streets and the vicinity of the factories, and contrasts too between the opinions of local residents and those of people interested in the factories and lorries. Difficult though it can be to collect realistic evidence on such matters, the attempt to do so gives far more purpose to the activity than can be found in the mere exercise of recording and mapping that sometimes passes as local studies. Clear use of key concepts gives some point to what is planned and some incentive to choose what are, for this particular purpose, the best available instances.

Up to this point, the planning has been conducted only in the teacher's own mind and through his activity, including his discussions with colleagues and others. The children in his class have, it is true, been considered as a 'variable' but not as active collaborators in the design of the unit. Therefore, in deciding how the time may actually be spent, he may well think of how, once the general theme has been introduced, they may wish to involve themselves in the planning and implicitly to design their own 'emergent objectives'. So he is unwilling to plan too thoroughly. The pursuit of autonomy as an aim would in any case be violated if a teacher were to prescribe everything in advance, however interesting it might be, with military precision. An element of open-endedness is necessary.

For the rest, a unit must take account of what the children are likely to be able to do, and to want to do, for although they will be fellow-workers, they will be neither adults nor angels. Decisions about their capabilities have to be taken by each individual teacher, bearing in mind the range of approaches and techniques which are nowadays available to a teacher. Section 2.3 takes up the discussion at this point, indicating some ways of organising units which the Project Team has found particularly useful.

Example 2
With a twelve-year-old class. The second example will be outlined much more briefly, since the process of decision-making by the teacher has been indicated in the first. This brief summary may itself suggest a useful format for similar purposes.

Children: mixed, wide ability range, some immigrants, one year's work in history and geography as separate subjects.

Teacher: specialist historian, with particular knowledge of and interest in modern History.

School: comprehensive; departmental organisation; wide range of facilities; emphasis on opportunity for as many children as possible to prepare for public examinations.

Environment: medium-sized town; school on outskirts; shows evidence of phases of growth since 16th century.

Possible theme suggested by teacher: The Victorians

Objectives that are most directly promoted

Intellectual skills 1, 4, 5: finding information, evaluating information, concepts and generalisations

Social skill 5: Empathy

Personal qualities 1, 2, 5: curiosity, wariness of over-commitment, interests

Key concepts selected for emphasis: communication, continuity/change

Use of social disciplines as resources: Communication and continuity/change, together with the emphasised objectives and the four variables, suggest focusing on:

    Victorian railway-building

    Victorian shipping

    The invention of the telegraph

    The beginnings of the popular press

Extension from History to the other disciplines suggests:
How the growth of communication in Victorian times
affected the Empire.
How change in communication was associated with the
disappearance of the Empire, and with what followed[7].
How we communicate with each other etc.
This is where relevant specific concepts can also be worked
out; for example, survey, travel, newspaper, missionary.
Design of a unit: Objectives and key concepts suggest
emphasis on the raising of pertinent questions and on com-
munication between children whose own attitudes to the
Victorians and the Empire may differ radically.

The Project's published units, and *Themes in outline*,
afford many examples of this kind of planning. Each published unit has its own Teacher's Guide in which the process
of planning in that instance is clarified. For teachers engaged
in planning for themselves, these can serve as examples, as
temporary guides, even as reserves of actual material to be
drawn upon until teachers build up for themselves something
more directly pertinent, on the lines suggested in section 3.1.

In the end, however, like the Project's table of objectives
and list of key concepts, units should be re-adapted by
teachers themselves. All of these are in a sense crutches, to
be discarded in due course when the process of thinking
deeply, systematically and reflectively about curriculum
planning has reached a stage at which this abandonment
becomes justified. In fact, to judge from the Project's work
with teachers, there may well be three phases through which
they pass:

1 Learning about the use of objectives and key concepts
and subject disciplines as resources, while making marginal
adaptations in their present curriculum.

2 Becoming familiar with the Project's objectives and key
concepts and applying them more fully and extensively, and
with growing confidence, in curriculum planning.

3 Adapting objectives and key concepts to their own
situation and building up units and banks of data and
information in accordance with their own considered needs.
This development may sound like a luxury for a country in

times of economic hardship. Looked at in a more penetrating way, it is nearer to a necessity, for a part of the nation's future depends on the purposive involvement of children during the middle years in the effective study of Man in Place, Time and Society.

References

1 See for example Tyler, Ralph W. *Basic Principles of Curriculum and Instruction*. Chicago, University of Chicago Press, 1949 (and re-issued as an Open University Set Book in the U.K. in 1971). Tyler's classification, in this seminal little book, was itself clear and purposive but it has become submerged in the course of more recent developments in curriculum studies.

2 A useful survey of some of these issues can be found in Bruner's own classic study. See Bruner, J. S., Goodnow, Jacqueline J. and Austin. G. E. *A Study of Thinking*. New York, John Wiley, 1957, especially chapters 2, 3 and 8. Chapter 3, on 'The process of concept attainment', has been reprinted as Chapter 8 of Bruner, J. S. *Beyond the Information Given*. London, Allen and Unwin, 1973.

3 Taba, Hilda, *Social Studies Curriculum Teachers' Guides*. Menlo Park, Calif., Addison-Wesley, 1969.

4 Bruner, J. S. *Towards a Theory of Instruction*. Cambridge, Mass., Belknap Press, 1966, chapter 4 and especially p. 74. See also Rudduck, Jean, 'Man: A Course of Study'. *Cambridge Journal of Education*, 2.2, Easter 1972, pp. 118–126, and for an analytical comment, Adams, Anthony, 'M.A.C.O.S. revisited' *Cambridge Journal of Education*, 4.3, Michaelmas 1974, pp. 104–113.

5 Entwistle, H. *Child-Centred Education*. London, Methuen, 1970, especially Chapter 5.

6 If it were a middle school 8–12, the situation would not be radically different. A 9–13 school could, however, alter the variable considerably since the children would be new to the school and the school itself might (not necessarily would) be less like a junior school in its social climate.

7 See section 1.5 above for a comment on the importance of relating historical material to the circumstances of today.

2.3   Implementing objectives: procedures

In section 2.1 (page 75) mention was made of the two special qualities emphasised by the Project. These are:
  critical thinking
  empathy
The present section will consider ways in which these special qualities can be encouraged in children between the ages of eight and thirteen. This will be done by using illustrative examples from the Project's work in schools. The examples chosen will highlight, in turn, learning experiences designed to foster the qualities and consider, in particular, the crucial role of the teacher in this process.

The development of critical thinking, and empathy, will depend a great deal on the quality of the interaction between children and teachers. Dearden[1] describes a kind of liberalised teaching which coincides, to a great extent, with the Project Team's views. Referring to liberalised teaching, Dearden says,

'It questions, discusses, sets tasks, hints, preserves judicious silences, prompts, provokes, invites contradiction, feigns ignorance, poses problems, demonstrates, pretends perplexity, comments, explains, and so on through a battery of devices by means of which passivity in intellectual learning may be overcome and a more critical learning stimulated. And as it succeeds, so independence of the teacher is gained and a more valuable self-direction becomes possible'.

A teacher operating in this way is constantly diagnosing the level of thinking of the child and choosing strategies to meet the situation. A major tool in the probing and diagnosis that takes place is the question the teacher asks. Teachers have been called 'professional question makers'[2]. There is, however, considerable evidence that teachers tend to ask questions that require short answers and factual recall more frequently than they ask questions which encourage the higher level skills of using facts, generalising and evaluating[3]. Much of the work on the way in which teachers use questions has been done in America. Most of the early work concentrated on investigating the social climate of a classroom and upon devices used to control this. Only recently has attention been turned to the role of teachers' questions in developing cognitive skills[4]. There are numerous systems for classifying teachers' questions, many of them stemming from Bloom's taxonomy so that there are questions

1 requiring the *recall* of knowledge,
2 encouraging the *application* of knowledge,
3 requiring *analysis*,
4 requiring *synthesis*
5 encouraging *evaluation*.

Such systems for the classification of questions can become too complex to provide practical guidance to busy teachers. Some classifications assume a teacher or instructor/large group relationship. Some assume small group interaction. Often the word 'discussion' is used interchangeably with the phrase 'questioning technique' and the two terms become inextricably confused.

The Project Team believes that teachers will find some of the American systems, at the best, too highly structured and at the worst, intolerably prescriptive. An attempt has been made to devise a system of classification of questions that avoids these problems. It is hoped to suggest a framework which will encourage teachers to analyse the questions they ask regardless of the context in which they are asked. Such a framework must satisfy the following criteria:

1 The system must be flexible enough to use either with small groups (which to the Team is preferable) or in groups of class size (which is all too often the reality).
2 The system must also provide guidance to teachers who are keen to devise their own assignment or work cards for their children. The written question, once formulated, cannot be adjusted or replaced in the way that the question put in discussion can be. But, if work cards are to be used and are seen as a useful device for overcoming the problem of numbers then the questions asked on these work cards can certainly go beyond the mere demanding of recall of information.
3 There must be a relationship between the kinds of questions asked and the objectives of the teacher.

Teachers' questions and critical thinking
It would be possible to produce a single sentence definition
of critical thinking but it is almost certainly more helpful to
consider the range of skills that children need to learn in
order to develop this special quality.

In the first place, critical thinking is founded on *curiosity*
which, if reference is made to the Project's table of objectives,
will be found to figure significantly in the list of personal
qualities. Teaching with an emphasis on telling and providing children with explanations will probably lead to a
situation where thinking for oneself is a chore. Teaching
which encourages a questioning attitude and a challenge to
look again at things that are taken for granted is likely to
foster curiosity. Curiosity is likely to be aroused and encouraged by presenting children with discrepant information
such as situations in which different individuals or groups
perceive the same event or issue. Newspaper accounts by
different eye-witnesses are a useful starting point with this
in mind. Children are prone to take for granted many of the
things around them. They are likely, for example, to make
assumptions that some jobs are only done by men and some
only by women. In an effort to encourage children to question
these assumptions some teachers working with the Project
have presented children with cartoon situations in which
traditional sex roles have been reversed. In a *Book of Social
Surprises* boys are shown playing with dolls, girls are shown
playing soldiers, and women are shown doing heavy manual
work. The valuable questions here are 'Why?', or 'Why not?',
and 'What do you think?'

Other important pre-requisites for critical thinking are
efficient ways of finding information from a variety of
sources and selecting, interpreting and evaluating information. Evaluating information requires being wary of biased
evidence or insufficient evidence to make a judgement.
Critical thinking also requires an ability to put tentative
ideas or explanations to the test by formulating and testing
hypotheses. For children 8 to 13 this does not mean setting
up and testing an elaborate network of hypotheses which is
characteristic of the university researcher but it does involve
children in the essential beginnings of that process. For

example, a group of junior school children in conducting a survey into the opinions of local people about moving to a nearby new town had found it widely believed that the price of food was more expensive in the new town than in the area from which they were moving. By a series of simple hypotheses the children were able to put these beliefs to the test.

From this it can be seen that critical thinking is a special quality that cannot be achieved through the pursuit of a single objective but is likely to be the result of organising experiences based on a battery of interdependent intellectual, social and attitudinal objectives. (See section 2.1).

It is also not a question of children acquiring one skill before moving on to the next. As children work on well planned themes they will be using a range of skills such as finding and interpreting information, evaluating and hypothesising. Progression in learning will involve moving to more sophisticated levels of using this combined range of skills.

The role of the teacher in fostering critical thinking is best explored by using an example. Children, aged about ten, were told a story of a man called Rawcliffe who used to live in a village called Bradley. He had died and the house in which he had lived was now derelict. Rawcliffe had a reputation as a recluse. Part of the interaction that took place after the telling of the story is analysed in terms of the questions the teacher asked.

When two children searched the derelict house they found several pieces of evidence. These were:

1 Some old coins
2 A broken chess piece
3 The corner of a playing card
4 An old pipe
5 A discharge certificate from the First World War showing that Sergeant Rawcliffe had been injured and honourably discharged on a date in 1918.
6 A dated newspaper cutting reporting the death of Mrs. Mary Rawcliffe (Rawcliffe's wife).
7 A dated newspaper cutting of the funeral of Miss Jane Rawcliffe, aged eight, the daughter of Henry Rawcliffe.
8 A letter (dated) to Rawcliffe, signed from 'your loving

sister', expressing concern over the illness of Rawcliffe's daughter.

How far could these young children distinguish between evidence definitely related to Rawcliffe and evidence that may or may not be connected with him? How far could they begin to answer the question 'Why do you think Rawcliffe was a recluse?' How far could they evaluate the evidence?

Their teacher began by asking a series of *closed questions* which demanded simple recall of the facts of the story.

Was Rawcliffe a soldier?
What were the names of the children in the story?
Why were they staying in the village?
What was the name of their uncle?
Who did they ask about the derelict house?

These are the kinds of questions which teachers recognise as establishing a baseline for further activity. They can predominate and result in concentration on low level skills.

The next set of questions used by the teacher were still closed – there was still only one set of acceptable answers but they did challenge the children to use some of the specific facts of the story. They are summed up in the question: can you put the events that occurred after Rawcliffe left the army in the order in which they happened? The group of 9 and 10 year olds in question were able to do this without much trouble.

When the teacher's questions turned to the relevance of the non-documentary evidence (the coins, the chess piece etc.) and they were asked to go beyond the data, their responses were less clear. The questions asked were:

Did Rawcliffe play chess?
How do you know?
Did Rawcliffe smoke a pipe?
How do you know? etc.

Some of the 9 and 10 year olds were very ready to make the assumption that if a pipe was found in Rawcliffe's house then Rawcliffe smoked and applied this when considering the relevance of the other objects. Two of the children saw that the presence of these objects in the man's house did not necessarily mean that they were his. Their reasoning began to infect the rest of the group. The interaction at this point was as follows:

T.	Do you think that he smoked, Angela?
Angela:	I don't know. He might have. My aunty has ashtrays all over her house and she doesn't smoke.
T.	Did he play chess?
Jackie:	He might have played with his daughter. I don't know.
Angela:	You can't tell.
T.	Is there any way we could find out for certain whether he played chess?
Roy:	You could go to his house again and see if you found a few more pieces and a board.
Jackie:	They still might be his daughter's.
Angela:	You can't tell. He might have, he might not.

Even Angela and Jackie, the two members of this group of children who saw most clearly the limitations of the objects as evidence about Rawcliffe, gave little indication that they were capable of treating the objects together as one set of limited evidence compared with the documentary evidence. The two girls made separate propositions about each object, i.e. He might have played chess, he might not. He might have played cards, he might not. These children were however, under the guidance of a sensitive teacher, gaining confidence in handling situations in which there was no certainty and no one correct answer, in ways often not found in much older children.

When asked 'Why was Rawcliffe a recluse?' 'Why did he keep to himself?' the children thought that he would be sad and lonely because of his rather tragic experiences which they had pieced together from the documents. They were able to empathise with the character. They were not able, and were not pressed by the teacher to try, to make a clear evaluation of the usefulness of the two kinds of evidence with which they were presented and did not go on to consider the process they were engaged in and its potentiality for transfer to other situations involving other characters.

116

Table 3 suggests a way of analysing some of the questions asked by the teacher and relates these to the objective of encouraging critical thinking. The questions are firmly related to the intellectual skill objectives but throw the emphasis on the higher level skills of evaluating evidence and formulating and testing hypotheses. A distinction is made between closed and open questions although it is appreciated that there is no such thing as a completely open question. All questions are to some extent based on assumptions about what is important and are therefore to some degree, directive. Closed questions are ones which call for a single or a predicted answer. Open questions encourage the children to go beyond what is given and what is known and seek children's opinions and evaluations. That young children find going beyond the evidence difficult is not disputed[5] but it is the experience of the Team that constant exposure to questions which ask them to do just that yields promising results. It is not being claimed that all closed questions are inferior and undesirable. There is a time and place for demanding the recall of specific facts and for encouraging children to classify and order facts they have learned. Indeed, classifying and ordering are basic operations in the formation of concepts[6]. It is also possible to have questions which demand classification and ordering that are a great deal more open than the example in the table. What is being claimed is that the kinds of questions teachers ask condition the kinds of thinking displayed by children. A piece of self-analysis and categorisation of the questions asked either orally or in writing can be revealing. If a predominance of closed questions is found then redressing the balance by asking some open questions will bring worthwhile results.

Another factor crucial to the development of critical thinking is the general atmosphere or social climate of the classroom in which the questioning takes place. An accepting atmosphere must prevail otherwise children will not readily expose their ideas and opinions. Such an atmosphere is fostered through every little interchange between teacher and child. It is based on the assumption by the teacher that every child has something worthwhile to say, even if he cannot articulate it very well. The quality of critical thinking is thus

Encouraging Critical Thinking through Questions

Table 3

A suggested framework on which to base an analysis of a teacher's questions

Closed Questions		Open Questions		Critical thinking
Demanding recall	Encouraging classification and ordering	Encouraging the use of data to draw conclusions	Encouraging awareness of the limitations of the evidence or evaluation of evidence	Encouraging an awareness of the processes of reasoning being used.
examples What were the names of the children in the story? Who were they staying with? What was the name of the man who had lived in the derelict house?	*example (closed)* Can you put the events in the order in which they happened? *example (less closed)* Can you think of a way or ways of sorting out the events in the story?	*examples* Did Rawcliffe play chess? How do you know? Did Rawcliffe smoke a pipe? How do you know?	*examples* What do we know for certain about Rawcliffe? What are we not so sure about?	*examples* How did we go about finding what kind of man Rawcliffe was? What different kinds of evidence did we use to find out about Rawcliffe? Were some bits of evidence more useful than others?

not solely an intellectual activity but has an important affective dimension which is supported by the social climate of the classroom created to a large extent by the teacher. The degree to which the teacher's style is directive (or non-directive) and supportive needs to be taken into consideration when interpreting the table. (See table 3)

The teacher's questions in this example play an important part in his overall strategy, i.e. to encourage the children to evaluate evidence and display some of the characteristics of critical thinking. The teacher's strategies lead the children through pathways to critical thinking. (See figure 5).

A fuller treatment of this topic will be found in *Teaching critical thinking skills*[7], one of the Project's publications.

Teaching for empathy
In the Project's table of objectives, social skill 5 is 'The ability to exercise empathy'. Empathy is defined as the capacity to understand another person's behaviour on the basis of one's own experience and behaviour and on the basis of information about the other's situation. Empathy has both a cognitive and an affective dimension. To exercise empathy involves being objective enough to understand another's point of view without necessarily agreeing with it. It also involves having sufficient sensitivity 'to feel' into another's situation. As many young children are characteristically egocentric they will have some difficulty in exercising empathy. Despite this, the Project Team has actively

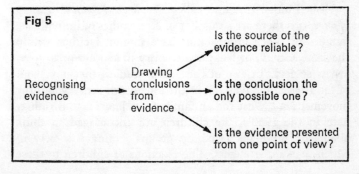

Fig 5

Recognising evidence → Drawing conclusions from evidence →

Is the source of the evidence reliable?

Is the conclusion the only possible one?

Is the evidence presented from one point of view?

encouraged teachers to provide opportunities for 8 to 13 year olds to empathise. In most cases this meant new experiences for both teachers and children. The responses have been promising and although it is difficult to design a test to prove that a child is empathising, if the evidence is taken from what children have written and said when asked to empathise, it appears that many of them have displayed this quality[8].

In encouraging empathy the Project's teachers have found the techniques of role play and simulation to be valuable. Details of some of the simulations developed by the Team can be found in *Games and simulations in the classroom*[9] which is one of the Project's publications. In addition, a more detailed coverage of the potential of empathy in the classroom will be found in *Teaching for empathy*[10].

Simulations aimed at encouraging empathy require children
a to assess as accurately as possible how another person or group sees a situation, and
b to select the elements in an often complicated situation that are related to the way another person or group appears to be seeing that situation.

Something is known about how the capacity to empathise develops within the family and peer group relationships but less is known about the effects on the ability to empathise of specially structured classroom experiences[11]. There is also evidence on the development of stereotypes and ethno-centrism which may build up barriers to the ability to exercise empathy.[12]

Examples of materials aimed at developing the ability to exercise empathy can be found in some of the Project's published units. In a unit called *People on the move: a study of migration* there are a number of case studies of individuals, families or other groups that have migrated either within the same society, or from one country to another or to form a new society. In two of these case studies, the movement of the Irish into Liverpool in the nineteenth century and the movement of a West Indian family from Jamaica to Birmingham in the 1960's, the children are encouraged to think about the problems faced by groups joining a society in which they are strangers. The reactions of children to these materials will differ widely but it will be interesting to find out whether the children find it easier to empathise with the Jamaican family to whom they are introduced through family photographs and tape recordings or with the Irish, who are, in the main, presented through historical documents, drawings and official reports from the mid-nineteenth century.

The experience of the Team in using case studies such as these with children 8 to 13 suggests that personalising the accounts to take into consideration the children's capacity to cope with the concrete and the particular rather than a general social category of persons, i.e. Mr Jones the car worker, rather than car workers or the McKay family rather than 'the Irish', is more effective in encouraging empathy. This, of course, is the basis of the appeal of a great deal of children's literature and some text-books and is not in any way 'new'. The Project Team, however, wishes to emphasise the potential of such material to teachers who are interested in the active pursuit of empathy as an objective.

A further challenge faced by the teacher who is interested in encouraging children to empathise is the necessity of providing in a case-study or a simulation sufficient information about the social background of the persons involved – their values, their beliefs, their problems, their constraints – to enable the children to begin to appreciate how these people see the world. It is only when this information is communicated in a meaningful way to the children that they can begin to relate their own feelings and values to those of the people in the case study. The teacher's task here is to effect a balance in the children's reactions between the cognitive and affective elements in the situation, avoiding on the one hand, a 'cold' intellectual response to the people in the case study and on the other making sure that there is no sentimental indulgence[13].

Exploring values
Referring again to the Project's table of objectives, it will be seen that social skill 5, 'the ability to exercise empathy', is related to personal quality 3, 'the fostering of a willingness to explore personal attitudes and values'. Empathy, then,

can be a useful tool with which to explore personal values and expose differences in values between individuals and groups. The probing and questioning of the teacher, however, is as important an element in the exploration of values as it was shown to be in encouraging the evaluation of information. It must be made clear that exploring values has nothing to do with the indoctrination of children into accepting the teacher's or the school's values. Exploring values is solely concerned with finding out what individuals and groups think to be important or think worthwhile or think to be right or wrong.

In asking questions which explore values there can be no correct answer that receives the teacher's tick of approval and no incorrect answer that is marked with a cross. Young children are obviously influenced, directly and indirectly by the values of the adults with whom they are in daily contact. This cannot be avoided. A teacher, however, who wishes to explore values with children, must create the classroom climate in which this is possible, one in which the opinions of all members of the group on value issues are treated in the same way.

Some of the teachers with whom the Project has worked have been, at first, reluctant to explore values with young children. Some who thought that the activity was much more appropriate for older children, have been surprised, when encouraged to experiment, at the maturity of the responses of 8 to 13 year olds on value issues. Some teachers have expressed a need for guidance in framing questions which explore values and it is with this in mind that the framework in figure 6 is put forward.

The framework suggests four criteria used in the formulation of questions about values.
1 Economic: Is it worth it?
2 Moral: Is it right or wrong?
3 Prudential: Is it wise or unwise?
4 Aesthetic: Is it beautiful or ugly?

The six boxes around the edge show the sorts of things that are commonly examined in discussions about values. Sometimes it is not appropriate to use all four criteria in formulating questions but it becomes obvious which apply.

Fig 6 A framework for exploring values

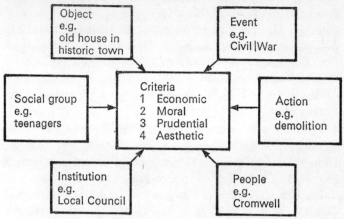

For example, in considering an act of demolition in a city centre one would ask (guided by the framework)

Is the demolition justifiable in economic terms?

Is the demolition right or wrong?

Will the demolition achieve our other objectives or not?

Will the demolition improve the beauty of the area?

Critical thinking, empathy and autonomy

It has been possible in this section to give only limited examples of the procedures employed to encourage critical thinking and empathy. It is clear that the teacher has a crucial role to play in these processes but, paradoxically, the more successful the teacher is the less crucial will become his role in relation to the child's learning because, to return to Dearden's words . . . 'as it (teaching) succeeds, so independence of the teacher is gained and a more valuable self-direction becomes possible'. In other words, critical thinking and empathy are seen as essential stages on the road to individual autonomy.

References

1 Dearden, R. F. *The Philosophy of Primary Education.* Routledge and Kegan Paul, 1968.

2 Aschner, M. J. 'Asking questions to trigger thinking' *N.E.A. Journal,* 1961, 50, pp. 44–46.

3 See, for example Pate, R. T. and Bremer, N. H. 'Guiding learning through skilful questioning' *Elementary School Journal*, Vol. 67, No. 8, May 1967, pp. 417–422.
Gall, M. D. 'The use of questions in teaching' *Review of Educational Research*, XL No. 5, Dec. 1970, pp. 707–721.
Both these papers and others on similar lines are reproduced in *Designing Instructional Strategies for Young Children*. Mills, B. C. and Mills, R. A., W. C. Brown, Dubuque, Iowa, 1972.

4 The most well known of these are Taba, Hilda, Levine, S. and Elzey, F. F. *Thinking in Elementary School Children*. United States Office of Education Co-operative Research Project, No. 1574, San Francisco State College, 1964.
Taba, Hilda, *Teaching Strategies and Cognitive Function in Elementary School Children*. U.S.D.E., Co-operative Research Project, No. 2404, San Francisco State College, 1966.

5 Peel, E. A. *The Nature of Adolescent Judgement*. Staples, 1972. Also 'Intellectual growth during adolescence.' Vol. 17. pp. 169–180. *Educational Review*, 1965.

6 Elliott, G. G. *Teaching for Concepts*, Collins, E. S. L. 1975.

7 Derricott, R., Waplington, A. *Teaching Critical Thinking Skills*. Collins, E. S. L. 1975.

8 Cooper, K. R. *Evaluation, Assessment and Record Keeping in History, Geography and Social Science*. Collins, E. S. L. 1975.

9 Elliott, G. G., Sumner, Hazel, Waplington, A. *Games and Simulations in the Classroom*. Collins, E. S. L. 1975.

10 Sumner, Hazel, *Teaching for Empathy*. Collins, E. S. L. 1975.

11 Weinstein, E. A. 'The Development of Interpersonal Competence'. Chapt. 17 in *Handbook of Socialisation Theory and Research*. Edited by Goslin, D. A. Rand McNally, Chicago, 1973.

12 LeVine, R. A., Campbell, D. T., *Ethnocentrism: Theories of Conflict, Ethnic Attitudes and Group Behaviour*. John Wiley and Sons, New York, 1972.

13 Jones, R. *Fantasy and Feeling in Education*. New York, New York Univ. Press, 1968.

2.4 The problem of sequence

A further dimension in curriculum planning, touched upon only briefly in preceding sections, is that of sequence. Deciding an order in which children are presented with the content of history, geography and social science is a task which teachers must face and one which has presented the Project Team with a problem.

Why has the sequencing of content presented a problem? Is it not possible to provide some generally acceptable rules for sequencing the content of history, geography and the social sciences? It could be argued that history has its own built-in sequence in chronology, which as it moves forwards, or backwards, in time determines automatically the order in which themes should be treated. In a similar way, the pattern for those learning geography is outwards spatially in ever increasing concentric circles. The starting point is the locality and the journey is to the distant, the remote, the exotic. With the social sciences the sequence could be from simple social situations often interpreted as small, face-to-face groups such as the family, to a study of groups and institutions of increasing complexity.

For the seeker after a universal sequence, there could surely be no clearer pattern. But in fact the pattern is far from clear. For example, even if history were only about chronology, there would still remain the problem of where on the great time chart to start and where to finish. The view that history is about change and about sifting and evaluating bits of evidence might be lost in such a treatment. Similarly, starting with the immediate and the accessible, whether it be the locality or the family, assumes a movement from the simple to the complex which might, in fact, not be valid, for the apparently simple is often more complex than it seems. Most families and most local communities have a sophisticated complexity which defies this much used sequencing principle.

If, then, there are shortcomings in the traditionally used approaches to sequencing by historians, geographers and social scientists, what alternatives can be considered? There is plenty of advice available. The writings on the sequencing of content are full of dogma, rhetoric, personal creeds and rule-of-thumb suggestions. Rarely is the tenuous nature of the relationship between a suggested sequence and its theoretical underpinnings openly admitted. Even when this is clearly enunciated, as for example in the Lawton Report on social studies[1], the tentative sequence suggested by a project team can still be perceived by a teacher looking for a lead from 'the establishment' as something very much more substantial than was intended: indeed, teachers have spoken in such terms about the Lawton Report to the Project Team. The problem then in writing on sequence is at least twofold; firstly, what is written may add to the mundane, confusing and generally unhelpful literature, secondly, that what is written either fails to communicate to teachers or assumes unwarranted authority in their eyes.

The importance of sequence was indicated in the drawing up of the Project's brief which said:

'Since there is, in spite of the range of individual differences among children, a substantial developmental interval between the ages of 8 and 13, involving the transition between two, and possibly three, schools particular attention should be paid to the question of *progression* in learning and especially to the relationship between development in children and the specific logical structures of history, geography and social science'.

Having set the task, which Hilda Taba described as one of the classical problems of curriculum organisation[2], the brief is helpful in defining the areas of operation that are likely to prove most fruitful in the search for sense about sequence. A rational sequence must be the result of the interaction between what is known about how children develop and what is valued – perspectives, skills, techniques – by historians, geographers and social scientists. This echoes Bruner's view that a theory of instruction should relate to a theory of development[3]. The Project Team also assume that there is 'no law of sequence' and that with the operation of the Four Variables 'accidental factors relating to historical traditions, personal inclinations and the availability of resources may properly be used to determine the

sequence of studies and that many different, equally satis
factory orders can be devised'[4].

Objectives and progression in learning
Reference to the Project's table of objectives will indicate
that it contains no specific knowledge objectives. This
means that there are no objectives related to specific bits of
knowledge such as – 'The ability to locate on a map of Norway
the principal fishing ports'. The emphasis is on the general
processing of information, i.e. finding, interpreting, com-
municating, evaluating, etc. The Project Team's work with
teachers has often led to experimenting with ways of providing progressive experiences through each of these
processes. Many of the experiences that were devised for
young children would be classified as *pre-disciplinary*. They
were not what the historian, geographer or expert in another
discipline might recognise as 'real' examples from within
their disciplines but they gave the children the opportunity
to practice skills and techniques used by the disciplines.

One of the intellectual skills from the table of objectives is
the ability to evaluate information. Historians, geographers
and social scientists look, in their different ways, for evidence
which they test for reliability and accuracy. The challenge
faced by the Project Team was to devise experiences of these
processes which would have meaning for young children.
Looking for and evaluating evidence can be put to children
as hunting for reliable clues. There are many sources outside
the disciplines of History, Geography and the Social Sciences
which can be used with young children. For example, when
Bill Shankly, the former manager of Liverpool Football Club
declares that a goal scored for Derby County against Liverpool was 'Definitely off-side', how reliable is his evidence?
This can be related to the opposing manager's view of the
same incident often demonstrating clearly that such evidence
can be biased. Similarly, how valid is the conclusion drawn
by Sherlock Holmes that a man suspected of a crime, who
has left a hat behind must be intelligent because he has a
large size in hats?

Experiences of this kind have been found appealing and
humorous by young children. Hunting for clues like these

127

may start at what some people might consider a trivial level but carefully sequenced experiences can accustom children to look at all evidence whether it be on the sports page of a newspaper or the findings of a sociological survey.

Further examples which use the device of progressing from pre-disciplinary material to authentic investigations within the disciplines can be found in the Project's published units. One of these units entitled *Clues, clues, clues: detective work in history* introduces the children to a number of pre-disciplinary activities before moving to sources from History. The sequence first presents the children with a well documented account of an actual crime then challenges them to solve a burglary at a house by examining the evidence found around the scene of the crime, before they are asked to work with evidence from historical documents and artefacts. Similarly, an analysis of the contents of a dustbin is used to provide some evidence of how a modern family lives before a case study of an archaeological dig of a Saxon hut is considered. This device of using techniques for evaluating information about the familiar, where the variables are controlled by the teacher, before using the same techniques on the unfamiliar, where the variables are less controllable, has proved useful in developing progression in learning.

Objectives, then, can be used to plan progression in learning *within* a chosen theme. A table of objectives can also be used as a checklist by teachers to ensure that, over a period of time, no one set of skills is being over emphasised and no one set underused or ignored. However, used in this way objectives do not provide any guidelines to the selection and sequencing of content. The planning of progression in learning based on skill objectives can be done with almost any content. It is with the task of selecting and sequencing content that key concepts have proved more useful.

Key concepts and sequence
The Project's seven key concepts are used as devices for helping to select and organise content. When using the key concepts with teachers the Project Team found the following sequencing principles useful as guidelines:

128

1 Emphasis on similarity/difference often precedes emphasis on continuity/change. Similarity/difference is seen as a basic concept-forming activity. Categorisation cannot begin to take place unless similarities and differences are first noticed. Therefore, in making decisions about sequence, similarity/difference will appear more often as a selecting and organising device than continuity/change with children in the early middle years.

2 When using comparison as a technique, such as, Then and Now or Here and There, *coarse* differences will appear before *fine* differences. Decisions about sequencing content should work on the basis that the younger the children are the stronger the contrasts need to be. The Team's experience in using key concepts confirms this. For example, in developing a theme on Shops with children of nine the teachers and the Team provided experiences and materials that contrasted the local, contemporary shopping pattern with shops and shopping in the same area in 1935 and in 1900. The stronger contrast with the earlier period was much more effective with these young children than that with the 1930's. The photographs, maps, written and oral accounts of shops in 1900 made a vivid contrast with the 1970's in a way which the same resources from the 1930's failed to do.

3 The younger the children the fewer the number of comparative elements used in any situation. It is also often desirable to precede an actual example of (say) differences in values between groups with a fictitious or simulated example in which the variables are closely controlled by the teacher. For example, in a theme on Leisure which encouraged children to find out local leisure needs and see how these were being met by decisions made to provide facilities, a simulation which showed how different groups could have different values about leisure and see the need for different facilities was a necessary preliminary to a study of the actual situation which was much more complicated.

Table 4 is a summary of the sequencing principles found to be useful when using the seven key concepts. The line between coarse and fine differences is, of course, not as

Table 4

Key Concepts and Sequencing Principles

Key Concepts	Coarse Differences	Fine Differences
Communication	Man moves from one place to another – cars, ships, planes, roads, canals – physical examples of communication before ...	Communication of ideas, press, radio, T.V., advertising, propaganda. Barriers to physical communication, barriers to communication of ideas.
Power	Power of man over physical elements, physical elements over man. Simulated examples before actual examples ...	Power of individuals over individuals, groups over groups. Decision making and power. Simulated followed by real examples.
Values and Beliefs	Strongly contrasting examples of what people think is important. Examples of values/beliefs about things, events, activities ... Emphasis on simulations ...	Economic, political and social values from simulated then actual case studies.
Conflict/ Consensus	Coarse disagreements, clear cut cases of conflict. Simple examples of reaching a consensus. Simulated examples of decision making ...	More complex examples of conflict over use of space, use of resources. Case studies of decision making.
Similarity/ Difference	Strong contrasting difference between then and now here and there them and us ...	Finer differences representing more subtle changes in place, time and society.
Continuity/ Change	Strongly contrasting examples of change e.g. before and after an event. Obvious examples of continuity ...	Increasingly more subtle examples of continuity/change.
Causes and Consequences	Situations with few interacting variables. Single causes – single consequences ...	Situations with more variables operating. Single causes – multiple consequences. Multiple causes – multiple consequences.

clear as this table makes it appear. It must also be emphasised that the suggested sequencing principles are not grounded in research but are the result of judgements made, with the benefit of hindsight, as the result of working with large numbers of teachers in many situations.

Some examples of sequences
The points made so far in this section about the use of objectives in planning for progression in learning and the use of key concepts to arrive at sequencing principles to be employed in syllabus construction are meant to encourage thinking about the problem of sequence. There is no ideal sequence in history, geography and social science which will be an appropriate blueprint for all circumstances. Each situation is unique, reflecting the needs of the children, teachers, schools and environments. All that can be provided here are ideas that may help teachers to make judgements about sequencing.

Approaches to sequencing in the middle years are particularly affected by the organisational structure of the education system. In practice, sequence is rarely considered between 8 and 13 but is more likely to be related to 7 to 11 or 8 to 12, 9 to 13 or 11 to 13. Although liaison on curriculum matters between stages, i.e. for example between junior and secondary schools or middle and third tier schools, is frequently held to be desirable, there is very little evidence that it takes place, a point which is raised again in sections 3.1 and 3.3. The consequences of these 'breaks' in schooling during the middle years are inconsistencies in approaches to sequencing. A third tier school may ignore, or be ignorant of, the existence of a carefully planned sequence in its contributing middle schools and proceed with its own ideas. A primary school may pay no attention to sequence at all and inadvertently introduce its children in the top years to the same themes that they will follow in the first year at the secondary school. Liaison which is aimed to avoid such situations is held by the Project Team to be essential.

Lack of liaison within schools and between schools can lead to children's experiences in history, geography and (where it applies) social science, being random and repetitive.

Themes can be chosen with few guiding principles in mind and repeated because teachers often do not know what has gone on before or what will go on later. Sometimes it is incredibly difficult to find out what goes on under the proliferation of labels attached to the activities in the Project's area of the curriculum. The Manchester Ship Canal can be studied under history, geography, social science, social studies, environmental studies, integrated studies, local studies, humanities, etc. The use of a guiding framework in curriculum planning of objectives and key concepts will not ensure that randomness and repetitiveness are avoided but, in the view of the Project Team, its use will go a long way towards reducing the possibility.

Some primary schools deliberately plan their history and geography schemes (under whatever label they choose to use) on a non-sequential basis. Often to the teachers in these schools, planned sequence means too much structure and too much direction of children's activities. These sincerely held views are respected and where adequate records are kept of the children's work, the children can gain a thorough grounding in study and reference skills. A non-sequential approach need not be random and repetitive and can result in the children mastering skills valued by historians, geographers and social scientists without the social subjects being on the timetable. The Project Team think, however, that this should not be left to chance. They believe that in the upper middle years the children should be introduced to the forms of knowledge that are represented by History, Geography and the Social Sciences and that this is best done by pursuing objectives and using key concepts central to these disciplines. Again, this does not necessarily mean using the subject labels fully for these activities. Some teachers with whom the Project has worked have implemented this approach by constructing a sequence which allows for some themes to be tackled from the viewpoint of one of the Project's disciplines in the final year in a junior or a middle school.

This section is illustrated by providing three examples of sequence. Each sequence is accompanied by an explanatory rationale. Each is the response to a unique situation and may appear to outsiders not involved in the planning, to be an arbitrary collection of themes.

Sequence A

As in all groups the teachers involved were constrained by the potentiality and limitations of the environment as a resource, as well as being influenced in their choice of themes by the bank of book and non-book resources they had gathered, with patience, over the years.

The group used the social subjects, particularly history and social science, as resources throughout the whole scheme. Their intention was to 'integrate' as they judged this the most appropriate way for them to organise learning experiences for their children.

The essential feature contained in sequence A is that the themes are chosen and put into an order without reference to key concepts. It is only when the order of the themes has been decided by judging their relevance and meaning to the children that the key concepts come into play. As suggested in section 2.2 these teachers use key concepts to help select, organise and focus content within a theme. There are three points worth making about the sequencing.

1 The themes in the early part of the sequence (i.e. for 8 and 9 year olds) are mainly concerned with people, places and things that the teachers assess as being within the experience of the children. The work on the Bushmen and to an extent that on farming are deliberately chosen to move the children's focus from the local and the immediate to wider issues.

2 There is a deliberately decreasing amount of local bias in the themes for the later years. The teachers see these as having potential for introducing the children in a more systematic way than earlier to the focus given by the disciplines. Thus, 'Children 100 years ago' is mainly historical, 'Money' relies mainly on the social sciences and 'South America' is mainly geographical.

3 It will be noticed that the teachers have chosen to emphasise two or three key concepts in each theme except in the case of the last two themes, 'South America' and 'Great Britain and Europe'. Similarity/difference occurs more frequently in the earlier part of the sequence and

Sequence A

Table 5

Age	Term 1 Theme	Term 1 Key Concepts	Term 2 Theme	Term 2 Key Concepts	Term 3 Theme	Term 3 Key Concepts
8+	Children's games, songs and pastimes	Communication Similarity/ Difference Continuity/Change	The family	Similarity/ Difference Continuity/Change Values/Beliefs	A non-literate society – the Bushmen	Similarity/ Difference Values/ Beliefs
9+	The local community	Communication Continuity/ Change	Going to school	Continuity/ Change Values/ Beliefs	Farming	Similarity/ Difference Continuity/Change Conflict/Consensus
10+	Workers and local industry	Power Similarity/ Difference Continuity/Change	Leisure	Conflict/Consensus Similarity/ Difference Continuity/Change	Living in Towns	Power Conflict/Consensus Similarity/ Difference
11+	Children 100 years ago	Continuity/Change Causes and Consequences	Money	Power Values/Beliefs Similarity/Difference	Rich and Poor	Power Conflict/Consensus Causes and Consequences
12+	The Second World War	Conflict/ Consensus Causes and Consequences	S. America	Power Conflict/Consensus Values/Beliefs Causes and Consequences	Great Britain and Europe	Power Conflict/Consensus Continuity/Change Causes and Consequences

causes and consequences appears in the later themes. This is not to be interpreted as meaning that an exploration of causes and consequences with young children is inappropriate. The inadequate explanations of causality given by children in the early middle years can provide a basis for fruitful interaction between teacher and child. However, from the evidence of the way thinking develops, an emphasis on causality is probably more appropriate in the later middle years.

4 It will also be noted that all seven key concepts in the Project's original list come under consideration at some stage between eight and thirteen.

Sequence B

The teachers who drew up sequence B have a different starting point. This group of teachers begins by considering the aims of education and finding for the teaching of history, geography and the social sciences, that the notion of key concepts helps them to move from aims to the selection and sequencing of content to fulfil these aims. Sequence B, then, is an example of the use of key concepts both to *select* and to *organise* content. The processes they followed in arriving at sequence B were as follows:

1 A recognition that the four substantive key concepts
   communication
   power
   values/beliefs
   conflict/consensus
   represent at a high level of abstraction important ideas which are the concern of historians, geographers and social scientists.

2 At the same time these four substantive key concepts are seen by the teachers as having general social and educational significance.

3 The three methodological key concepts
   similarity/difference
   continuity/change
   causes and consequences
   also have application to the subject area of the Project and represent general processes which are at the basis of enquiry or habits of scholarship.

Sequence B — Substantive Key Concepts

Table 6

	Communication	Power	Values/Beliefs	Conflict/Consensus	Methodological Key Concepts
8+	Transport in a local setting. Local road patterns. Local transport services.	Preserving law and order. The Police Service past and present.	Rules: safety rules, highway code, rules in games. Belonging to groups with rules, Scouts, etc.	Simulation: setting up an Island Society	Similarity/Difference
9+	National network of motorways. Railways. Airports. Why is the pattern as it is?	Simulation: The siting of a new airport. Who decides?	Families in different cultures. Comparison of roles of individuals in families.	Conflict over the use of domestic space, local space.	
10+	Barriers to communication and how these are overcome. Crossing rivers, estuaries. Tunnels, the Channel Tunnel.	Floods: living with the threat of floods.	Going to school. Ways in which the young are taught in different cultures.	Providing for leisure need – conflicts of interest. Tourist v. Conservationist.	Continuity/Change
11+	Communication through the media. Newspapers, radio, T.V.	Working in a factory. Trades Unions. Strikes.	Victorian life.	Life during the Second World War.	Causes and Consequences
12+	Advertising. Can we believe all we are told?	The Oil Crisis. Who has the power?	Culture clash. The Aborigines of Australia.	Enclosures: Simulations.	

4 Sequence B evolved from the teachers taking the four substantive key concepts and deriving from them themes and experiences which they considered appropriate to illustrate at each age level from eight to thirteen.

Communication is illuminated by ideas that move from local transport, through national transport to physical barriers to communication (estuaries). The communication of *ideas* through the media is not considered until the later years.

Power is also considered at first in a local setting and moves through a simulation to decision making. The theme of 'Floods' is introduced to explore the idea of the dangers man faces from natural disasters and how man tries to control his environment to avoid disasters. Trade Unions and the oil crisis were thought to be two topical and significant themes through which to further elaborate on the key concept of power.

Values and beliefs are dealt with by developing themes which until the last two years of the sequence, are rooted in the child's own experience. Similarly *conflict/consensus* begins with the children's drama by simulating an Island Society and remains within the immediate and the local by looking at conflicts over the use of domestic and local space before moving on to more general themes.

The use of the methodological key concepts is similar to that in sequence A. In the early middle years the emphasis is on similarity/difference moving later to continuity/change and causes and consequences.

The substantive key concepts in this sequence are used to give children experiences of people and groups who have different values and to encourage the exploration of the children's own values. This is often done through simulations as in the Airport simulation and the Enclosure simulation but it is also tackled through a study of the Victorians which emphasises values and beliefs and through the Culture Clash theme which focuses on the Aborigines.

Sequence C

This is an example of a sequence which was designed for the first two years (11 to 13) in a comprehensive school. As is so often the case the teachers in this school were facing not one

Sequence C   Table 7

138

Age	Content	Key Concepts	Sequencing Principles		Terms
11+	Liverpool – city of change. Emphasis on physical changes – planning	Communication Continuity/Change Similarity/Difference	Near spatially Near socially Near in time *Familiar*	Emphasis on intellectual skills 1, 2, 4 Social skill 2	1
	Liverpool – social changes, patterns of immigration, Irish, Welsh, W. Indians, Chinese.	Conflict/Consensus Continuity/Change Similarity/Difference	Near spatially Near socially *Less familiar*	Emphasis on intellectual skills 1, 2, 3, 4 Physical skills 1, 3 Social skill 2	2
12+	Liverpool and the Slave Trade	Values/Beliefs Power Continuity/Change	Near spatially Distant in time *Sensitive*	Intellectual skills 2, 3, 5 Social skill 3	3
	South Africa and the Boer War	Causes and Consequences Power Conflict/Consensus Continuity/Change	Distant spatially Distant in time	Intellectual skills 2, 3, 5, 6 Social skill 5 Physical skills 2, 4	4
13+	South Africa today	Causes and Consequences Power Values/Beliefs Similarity/Difference	Distant spatially Near in time Distant socially *Sensitive*	Intellectual skills 3, 5, 6 Social skill 5	5
	Liverpool – a multicultural society?	Causes and Consequences Conflict/Consensus Values/Beliefs	Near spatially Near in time Near socially *Sensitive*	Intellectual skills 3, 5, 6 Social skill 5	6

change but many. They were moving from subject to integrated studies, from streaming to mixed ability, from class teaching to collaborative or team teaching, they were also interested in developing their own resources centre.

In the past they would have started with subjects, in this case, history and geography. Now they were concerned to use the corresponding academic disciplines and experiment with social science to produce what they thought to be a relevant 'integrated' course for the first two years of the school which would form a sound basis for work in the upper part of the school which was mainly subject centred and for most of the children, aimed at public examinations. The decision was taken to centre on the local community, its roots and its development. Teachers felt that a focus on the local community was important but could be a narrowing experience, so they deliberately chose to explore with the children contrasting communities both in time (Slave Trade, Boer War) and in place (South Africa Today).

Sequence A and sequence C were both evolved without initial reference to key concepts. However, the theme running through sequence C is that of Change. It begins with the motto 'Liverpool, city of change and challenge' and explores aspects of change. The starting point is observable physical change, changes in landscape, changes in the inner urban area, changes in the central shopping area. It moves on to less obvious aspects of change – patterns of immigration. The key concept of values and beliefs is used to illuminate differences in values amongst various immigrant groups and its potential for conflict. Again, as in sequence B the key concepts open up the possibilities of examining differences in values and teaching valuing.

The chart tries to make explicit the sequencing principles employed by the group of teachers. It begins by moving from the familiar to the less familiar. One of the most interesting features is the way in which *sensitive issues* are sequenced. As values and beliefs become more central in the sequence the themes are likely to contain sensitive issues of relations between races. The theme 'Liverpool and the Slave Trade' is an attempt to introduce a potentially sensitive issue by distancing it in time. 'South Africa and the Boer War' introduces conflict at a distance and 'South Africa Today' brings this into a contemporary setting. It is only after these experiences that the final highly sensitive theme which asks the question 'Liverpool – a multicultural Society?' is tackled.

Another important strand in sequence C which distinguishes it from both A and B, is the attempt to *sequence skills*. The number after intellectual, social and psychomotor skills refer to the Project's initial list of objectives. These are the skills the teachers intend to emphasise in structuring the various themes. The higher level intellectual skills of evaluating evidence and formulating hypotheses and the social skill of empathy are emphasised in the later rather than the earlier themes.

Conclusion
One question that is quite likely to arise in teachers' discussions about sequence is this: What might children reasonably be expected to have 'done' in the social subjects before they reach the age of 13? This question is really about the skills, knowledge and attitudes which children could be relied upon to carry forward, in some measure, as equipment for study in the upper secondary years. This applies especially to those who are likely to take public examinations, for it would be unrealistic to ignore the prominence that these considerations understandably occupy in the minds of teachers.

In one respect, this question can be answered. If a range of objectives is pursued, then intellectual skill 3 in the Project's table (interpreting information) or its equivalent is likely to be included, and this involves a great many of the stock skills and terminologies of the social subjects. What is more, these skills and terminologies are likely, in the Project's approach, to have been learned in a meaningful context. The conventional time-scale and the notion of 'depth' in time, for example, will have been apprehended through an emphasis on continuity/change, the network of latitude and longitude in relation to communication, and terms such as 'imports' through considering oil in the light of power. Approaches such as these should lead to a reasonable initiation into the ways of thinking appropriate to the social disciplines, rather than to the rote learning of dates and locations and definitions, recalled with difficulty and reproduced with inaccuracy.

Meanwhile, the general distribution of the continents and oceans and of the place relations of many major centres are likely to have been quite extensively explored, always with some purpose such as their significance in relation to population movement or food supply. The meaning of terms such as 'mediaeval' or 'primitive' or 'kinship' too, will usually have been brought out through one unit or more. And since each sequence should be designed in a manner appropriate to particular situations in terms of the four variables, it should also be possible to build up an increasing familiarity with ideas of this kind as the years pass, without resorting to chronological or topographical 'coverage', for it is the growth of the ideas, not the ordering of the subject-matter, that constitutes the guiding principle of the Project's strategy. The use of a table of objectives as a checklist itself helps to bring to teachers' notice the importance of the development of ideas, though of course not necessarily the same ideas, in the same order, for all children.

For this reason, and indeed from this section as a whole, it is clear that if the question about children's attainments at the age of 13 refers not to skills and terminologies and interest and keenness but to actual content, then to the Project it must be literally unanswerable. Neither the Normans, nor the Temperate Grasslands, nor Division of Labour has an absolute, prescriptive right to be included. If the set of objectives used by teachers has been systematically followed between the ages of 8 and 13, they will have acquired during those years a very substantial range of actual knowledge, much of which they will retain because of the way in which it was originally encountered and subsequently built on: but their main legacy from the middle years will not be a knowledge base but an intellectual, social and personal equipment which they can then use for a more systematic and sequential study. In any case, such study is likely to be a new experience with a new quality, marking a new level of maturity. Whatever may be true of the sciences, mathematics or modern languages, there is little to indicate that study in the social subjects after 13 depends directly on specific content absorbed before that age. Understanding Gladstone, even if it is possible, does not necessarily depend on first understanding Henry VII. Issues of this kind have, of course, been explored by other Schools Council Projects such as *Geography for the young school leaver* and *History 13–16*, with both of which the Project has shared many ideas.

Thus sequence in the social subjects before the age of 13 should be strenuous and satisfying in its own terms, as the examples outlined in this section try to be. 'Coverage' is impossible, and self-defeating, while the definition of a necessary minimum content (except perhaps the intelligent use of the immediate environment in Place, Time and Society) is equally unrealistic. For the educational process is not a book to be read from cover to cover, but a life to be experienced, for its own sake, at every stage.

References

1 Lawton, D., Campbell, J., and Burkett, V. *Social Studies 8–13*, Schools Council Working Paper 39. Evans-Methuen, 1971.

2 Taba, Hilda. *Curriculum Development, Theory and Practice.* Harcourt, Brace and World, 1962.

3 Bruner, J. S. *Towards a Theory of Instruction.* Cambridge, Mass. Harvard Univ. Press, 1966.

4 Phenix, P. H. *Realms of Meaning.* New York, McGraw Hill, 1964.

2.5 Assessment, evaluation and record keeping

Assessment

Many teachers feel that the absence of any external examinations in middle schools and most junior schools, is a definite asset. It has allowed the teachers to develop curricula with a freedom which is not always possible in a secondary school. The pressures of G.C.E. 'O' level, C.S.E. Mode 1, and even C.S.E. Mode 3 examinations are certainly felt in the third year of many secondary schools, and in the first year of some. At the least, many teachers would be reluctant to deal in the first two years of the secondary school with content which is going to be covered again a few years later. Because the examination syllabuses are necessarily fixed in advance, this constraint will always operate against the teacher who, for whatever reason, would like to look at the content area to be covered for the examination, with classes lower down the school. The teacher in the junior school or the middle school, particularly when dealing with topics in the area of the social subjects, will not feel any such pressure.

At the same time, many teachers welcome external examinations as providing some outside check on what the pupils have learnt, and what the teacher has taught. The teacher is able to see the criteria by which he can judge the progress the pupils have made, and he is able to use the same criteria and techniques of testing to make his own checks before the examination. It is, for instance, very common for teachers to set some sort of mock or practice examination some time before the real one, and to use a past paper for this. The teacher can feel that he has a fairly clear idea of the pupil's standard of work. It might be debated as to whether this feeling is often illusion rather than reality, even for teachers involved with external examinations; what is clear is that teachers dealing with children 8 to 13 often feel unhappy that they haven't even got the illusion of assessing progress by an external standard.

This difficulty is undoubtedly increased by the subject area the Project is dealing with, and by the ways in which the Project has looked at it. Firstly, the Project has suggested that learning in this area be concept-and-skills-based rather than content-based. This means that the major aim is not to ensure that the children learn, and retain for as long as possible, a number of specific facts; it is to help the children to fit the facts into a wider understanding of the processes involved, so that they will be able to bring this understanding to other, more or less similar, situations. Secondly, the Project has stressed the idea the teachers might work towards the development in the children of an ability to think about their work in a deep and critical way. In the Project's table of objectives, this is exemplified by 'evaluation of evidence', and 'formulating and testing hypotheses'. Both these

143

characteristics of the Project are ideas about what children should be doing which it is sometimes difficult to put into words, let alone finding a way to estimate the pupils' progress towards achieving them in any meaningful or reliable way.

Built in to much of the teacher's unhappiness about not having some external standard against which to judge his pupils and himself, is the notion that such an external standard necessarily exists, and that our aim should be to try to measure student progress against it as accurately as possible. Much educational literature seems to have been devoted to persuading us that measurement equals hard evidence, which is very much more desirable and useful than any other (soft) evidence. It is not only teachers who have acquired this belief – it has to some extent been communicated to parents and children as well.

Evaluation

Most teachers want to evaluate the effectiveness of their own teaching – but very rarely do in any formal way. Few practising teachers follow the requirements of students on teaching practice in writing an evaluation of a lesson immediately afterwards. Few departments in secondary schools meet together at the end of the year to review the scheme of work in the light of the year's experience. The nearest most of us as teachers come to evaluating our own effectiveness is when we are confronted by the results of some external assessment of the pupils, and we discover how well the pupils in our class have done compared to some national standard. If only a third of the class achieve the appropriate score for their chronological age on the Schonell Reading Test; if only two out of thirty pass the 11+; if all the candidates we enter for 'O' level English Literature failed; then we are taken aback and seriously wonder where we went wrong. Even at this point, however, it is possible for the teacher to use this solely as evidence about the poor potential of the children, and not even consider the possibility of relating it to the quality of the teaching.

Where this external evidence is not available (as in most middle schools) the teacher is usually driven back to using two main sources of information to evaluate his own teaching.

Firstly, he can record the 'progress' of each child through the various graded schemes he uses, particularly in Maths, and Reading. He might try to get all the children up to Fletcher Book 6, or Ladybird Book 10, for instance. Secondly, the teacher frequently sets his own end-of-term or end-of-year tests. He soon finds that the difficulty with using these teacher-made tests for either pupil assessment or evaluation is that it is difficult to see how these tests compare to any particular standard – whether 50% on the test is good or bad, compared to the score that other children of the same age and ability might have achieved.

Record keeping

Some form of record keeping is one of the activities which seems to mark out the professions from other occupations. Medicine would be totally lost without the case-notes or the patient's medical record. Social work would be impossible without notes on visits and a record of the worker's actions. In education, however, records are frequently regarded as an activity to be avoided if possible, and performed in a minimal way if not. Perhaps this is because records are only worth doing if the records are going to be of use to, and used by, colleagues; currently the records which teachers are expected to keep are not used very much, and teachers quite reasonably resent spending time on a pointless exercise. The most persistent offender in this respect is the 'official' record card for each pupil which many authorities require schools to keep for each pupil. The information which is demanded is often very informative about the child's place in the family (how many brothers and sisters, with their ages and schools), but does not say much about whether the child is good at multiplication but not at division, or whether he is able to read silently. Many teachers do, of course, keep their own records of the child's progress through the year. The adequacy and use of these varies from teacher to teacher – but they are rarely passed on with the child, and there is often no mechanism for doing this.

Objectives as a key

So far the three strands have been looked at separately, because that seems to be the way in which they are treated at the moment. One of the interesting side-effects of the Project's trials, however, was that a number of the trial teachers became interested in finding a way of assessing the progress of the pupils in a way which would do justice to the approaches the Project was advocating. It seemed appropriate to look for a way to integrate the three activities, so that information used to assess pupils can also be used by the teacher to evaluate his own teaching; information used for evaluation can help in the assessment of progress; and record keeping becomes an essential aid to teaching, rather than a chore.

Although this was not originally seen as one of the functions of the evaluator, it was clear that the demand was strong, and that some of the approaches used in the overall evaluation of the Project would be helpful to the teachers in this respect. In particular, the idea of evaluation as providing information on the basis of which decisions can be made[1] is a possible starting point. If both assessment and evaluation are seen as the collection of information to use in making decisions (whether about teaching or about a pupil), then certain questions to be asked in any information-gathering situation come to mind.

1 What do I want to know?
2 Why do I want to know it?
3 What am I prepared to count as evidence?
4 How am I going to use it?
5 Is it really worth the effort?

A key to this possible integration of assessment, evaluation and record keeping could be the use of *objectives*. This has been discussed earlier in this book, and the full discussion need not be repeated here. The important point which needs to be made is that these objectives need not necessarily be specific behavioural objectives. It is true that the more specific the objective is, the more easily it can be assessed; but in the past this has led to an undue concentration on those specific objectives – particularly to do with recall of specific facts – which have been easy to frame. The teacher must feel that his objectives are those which most accurately reflect his own educational priorities for the children. At whatever level they are framed, however, the use of objectives does make assessment and evaluation easier. If we have some idea of what we hope the pupils will 'learn', it becomes more feasible to go on to ways of finding out how well individuals have 'learnt' it, and how well the teacher has 'taught' it. Let us take the Project's objective to do with the evaluation of evidence as an example. If we as teachers think this skill is important, then we will try to come to some understanding of what we mean by it. Suppose we decide that part of this skill as we understand it is the ability on the part of the children to be able to distinguish between fact and opinion. The statement of the problem in this way makes it immediately clearer how this might be assessed. It could be a pencil and paper test, where the child is required to pick out the statements of fact and the statements of opinion; it might be the assessment of a tape-recorded report made by a child when she was asked to find out how much of her own parents' views on local councillors are based on fact, and how much on opinion; or it might be that the teacher noticed that in a discussion in class one day Carol said, 'That's only his idea of what happened. He couldn't really know'.

If the teacher has as his objective the development of this particular skill by the pupils, then the results of each of these ways of assessment could be used to give him insight into his own teaching. Most important of all, perhaps, the question will be raised of how much opportunity the teacher has given the pupils to develop these skills. Has the teacher ever asked the children about the difference between fact and opinion? Has he ever accepted and reinforced contributions to discussion such as the one Carol made, and shown that he values them? Does he feel that Carol's remark is an important enough sign to her development that he is prepared to take time to write something about it – either a tick on a prepared form, or a brief note of the incident with a date? Can he see ways in which he can use Carol's new insight to develop this skill further, or to develop other, related, skills?

Both of these methods of record keeping really amount to the same thing. In the first, however, it is necessary for the teacher (or more usefully, for the department or all the teachers in the school) to make some list beforehand of the headings, or particular situations, which will count as important. For example, in one such list prepared for a particular school during the Project's diffusion phase (and set in an historical context), one section read:

Comprehension skills A child who has developed these skills can
    a give the essence of a piece of material he has read e.g. 'According to this book they were very poor in those days'
    b describe the main features of a piece of evidence e.g. 'Well, they went to school without breakfast, or without coats in the winter'.

Another list developed, using just the main headings of areas that the teacher would be interested in both for assessment and evaluation, had the following section:

Finding out
    Basic reading skill
    Comprehension
    Finding: use of index
            finding source
    Curiosity
    Observation: looking
               recording
    Interpreting: pictures
              graphs
              maps

Perhaps the first of these examples would be easier for the teacher to use as a checklist for the progress of each pupil, ticking off the item when a child had shown whether in oral work, in written work, or perhaps in painting or modelling, evidence of developing these skills. The second example might, as it stands, be more useful for the teacher to use in preparing work for the class, to make sure that important areas are being introduced, or as headings under which to make notes about observations he has made of the child's progress. The progress could again be shown in many contexts – written, oral, or any other[2].

Record keeping undertaken in these ways could have a twofold importance. Firstly, the teacher would have a base from which he could, with some confidence, plan work for individual children, since he has a reasonable idea of their strengths and weaknesses. This knowledge is, of course, already possessed by good teachers; but it is often kept in the teacher's head, which makes it difficult for the teacher to be sure that he has remembered everything of importance, and which makes it impossible for any other teacher to use this knowledge to save time in the child's later education. Secondly, the teacher has the information from which he can evaluate his own work – but at the same time the act of recording each child's progress will help the teacher to consider his teaching, and the opportunities he is providing for skill or attitude development.

References
1 Schools Council *Curriculum Evaluation Today – Trends and Implications*. Macmillan Education (Schools Council Research Series) 1975.

2 The idea of objectives-based assessment, evaluation and record keeping is developed more fully in the Project's support publication on this topic. (Keith Cooper: *Evaluation, assessment and record keeping in history, geography and social science*.) This is intended to be of practical help to teachers concerned with work in this curriculum area. Many of the techniques and ideas used there and in the present section derive from those employed in the evaluation of the Project. These in their turn were derived from a variety of sources; in particular, the notion of the checklist was adapted from that used by the evaluator of *Science 5–13*. See: Harlen, W. *Science 5–13: a Formative Evaluation*. Macmillan Education (Schools Council Research Series) 1975. This work was later developed in the Schools Council Project, *Progress in Learning Science*, directed by Dr. Wynne Harlen at the University of Reading.

2.6 Variations in approach

The preceding sections indicate the broad guidelines which the Project recommends to teachers engaged in curriculum planning for the social subjects 8–13. But it would be a mistake to imagine that there is necessarily any one best way for a teacher to approach the Project's ideas. By way of example, this final section exemplifies some of the differences in emphasis and acceptance which were shown by teachers working with the Project during the experimental and diffusion phases. There were a few teachers for whom one or more of the important ideas of the Project struck an immediate chord. After his initial introduction to working with the Project's ideas, one teacher wrote that the Project would be useful '. . . in making environmental study-type work less patchy from the point of view of important concepts, and will also help in re-thinking about fitting various skills into this type of work, i.e. bringing skills into a natural scheme of activities devised in observing the environment.' Others felt that the Project had managed to crystallise into words ideas towards which they themselves had been working. For this reason they found the Project very valuable.

The immediate reaction of the vast majority of teachers, however, is typified by the comment, 'although they have never been written down on paper, I feel that many of the objectives are already pursued at my school'. The initial starting point was therefore one of scepticism. After a period of contact with the Project's objectives and key concepts, however, the scepticism had in most cases been replaced by an acknowledgement of the value of at least one part of the Project's basic framework. One teacher in a middle school felt that the Project had really made her think about what she was doing 'for the first time since leaving college'. One teacher said that he had thought on initial contact that the ideas were 'crazy'; now he found them both useful and relevant, helping him to think about underlying skills rather than merely about content.

Indeed for most of those who did find value in the Project, it was the objectives which were of major importance. The key concepts were not given equal status by these teachers. One said, 'I've tried to make the key concepts important, but I don't think they are'. Another said that, while he found the objectives useful, the key concepts were merely 'interesting'. There were however, other teachers for whom the key concepts were the principal revelation. They saw them having great importance as the organising principle behind the selection and presentation of work for the children; the objectives were felt by some of these teachers to be rather pedestrian, while it was the key concepts which were an exciting innovation. A third category of teacher also emerged, who saw benefits in both the objectives and the key concepts, and for whom contact with the Project had been proportionately greater value. One of the main comments made by these teachers was that the Project's ideas were a good framework to use in teaching – a 'fine guideline' one said. The other frequent comment, particularly from experienced teachers, was that contact with the Project had made them realise that they had been consistently underestimating the children.

The Project has emphasised the uniqueness of every situation. It would therefore be surprising if every part of the Project's ideas were useful to teachers to the same degree. In no sense would 'all or nothing' be an appropriate slogan. Some teachers will find the whole of what the Project has to say to be relevant and useful; some will find it all trite, and some will consider it old hat. Most teachers will, on the basis of the reactions of teachers who have taken part in the Project's work, find at least some aspect of the ideas relevant and useful for the classroom in the first instance and may well discover hidden reserves in themselves which enable them to develop these ideas in ways which they think valuable. The Project, having provided the initial impetus, encourages them to develop further in their own way. Part 3 offers some suggestions about how they, together with those who find the Project's whole strategy more congenial, might achieve this.

Part three
The maintenance of
curriculum planning

Part 2 has indicated the ways in which teachers, individually and in groups, can think deeply, systematically and reflectively about curriculum planning in the social subjects for the middle years. The Project's published units and *Themes in outline* have been devised as examples of what can be planned, and the rest of the publications are intended to help teachers in their own planning. What remains to be considered in Part 3, in the light of the Project's diffusion programme, is how the process of curriculum planning itself can be sustained by teachers, teacher-educators, and administrators, for unless the process is effectively maintained, the main purpose of the Project will be impeded. Section 3.1 makes some suggestions about planning within schools, based on the Project's experience; sections 3.2 and 3.3 embody rather more tentative recommendations, still based as far as possible on the Project's experiences, about teacher education and administrative support.

3.1 Maintaining planning within schools

Whatever may happen elsewhere, it is within individual schools in ordinary circumstances and under ordinary pressures that this planning has to be carried out. During the diffusion programme, when the Project set up workshops for teachers, suspicions were often apparent that teachers had no time for luxuries like curriculum planning. Yet if a Project is to avoid the fate which Hoyle calls 'tissue rejection'[1], that is, if its ideas are not to be transplanted into a school situation and then fail to become part of the 'organism', some means must be found of convincing heads and also classroom teachers, and in secondary schools heads of departments, that the Project's approach has some value for them.

Starting

The most decisive step is the first. Somebody has to break with their previous practice and initiate something new in their own professional activity. It may be through encountering the Project's publications, including this book, which is itself intended to start people thinking. It may on the other hand be because of a personal contact through the Local Education Authority or through some other organisation, or through some other development not connected with the Project itself at all, such as a course or a book or a set of materials devised by somebody else[2].

Probably the first thing a teacher does is to think how these new ideas could be accommodated into his present style of teaching: would their adoption, for example, lead to an immediate widening of the scope of what is done, or would it also result in so great a disturbance of the existing programme of work that the risks involved appear daunting? This is a genuine question and one that may quite understandably lead to an initially sceptical, defensive stance towards the Project.

One form taken by this defensive stance is to think that the new ideas are not, after all, very new, and that they are already in use. Most of the workshops conducted by the Project revealed at least one teacher who reacted in this way. The explanation probably is that the tangible products of the Project's units do not look very different from the outcome of much that is already common practice in vigorous and effective junior, middle and secondary schools. It takes a little time to appreciate that the use of objectives and key concepts gives a firmer basis for these procedures. But even when objectives and key concepts are mentioned, teachers still often maintain that these too are already in use. What this often means is, however, that it is possible to take a theme or unit or topic already being followed with children and to label it with particular objectives or key concepts which seem, almost as an afterthought, relevant. This is what the Project Team once called, in one of its internal documents, the use of objectives and key concepts as 'flags of convenience'[3]. It is of course a quite different matter from using objectives and key concepts systematically in the selection of themes and the organisation of units.

This phase of legitimate scepticism has frequently been followed by a second in which a teacher gains a fuller realisation of what the Project is trying to do. Where the Team has been present, this could arise through discussion but during the diffusion phase there has been some indication, fortunately, that direct personal contact is not essential. It is at this point that a teacher can make a decision to innovate.

Having taken a decision to re-think the basis of work in the social subjects, a teacher could next take stock of what the school already possesses in books, non-book materials, apparatus and other resources such as corridors and corners where children can work in small groups and could also re-consider the potentialities of the social environment. Along with this it may be necessary for a teacher to begin to extend his own grasp on the social disciplines as resources, as suggested in section 1.3, whether or not he is already versed in one or more of them.

The third step is to consider whether any colleagues would be ready and willing to collaborate in a new venture in curriculum planning. The support of one or two colleagues, however informal in nature, can substantially extend the ideas and resources available to a teacher who is starting something new. It may involve more than this, since it is difficult to embark upon change in the face of opposition especially if it is expressed by those who are in authority; that is of course why schools, as well as teachers, figure in the Project's strategy as variables. On the other hand, if a small group of teachers with similar ideas are keen to work together in a more thorough-going way, this can lead to team teaching of a more definite nature, a point that will be considered later in this section.

In any case, it is necessary for any teacher or teachers to try to anticipate the impact which their re-thinking may have upon their colleagues. Obviously it cannot be assumed that they will always be willing to help, by sharing their official expertise in art or English or even in other aspects of the social subjects, or their unofficial interests in fell-walking or in reminiscing about their wartime experiences, or even

155

by looking after groups of children while others are out exploring the environment. Even apart from this there is the possibility of sceptical reaction among colleagues to any eager innovatory venture, especially if it is perceived as yet another in a long list of projects imposed by others. Before embarking upon curriculum planning, a teacher has to have some idea, on a practical level at least, of the ways in which schools, as organisations, behave[4].

Of particular importance, too, is the attitude of the authority figures in the school, the head and other senior members of staff. During the Project's school programme, some heads and others were enthusiastic, some benevolent, some cool, but none hostile because then the Project would not have been established in the school at all. Such heads might, however, exist elsewhere. Meanwhile, one or two regarded the Project as a useful way of inducing their heads of department to alter their approach; this raised some delicate questions for the junior staff directly involved with the Project.

Planning
Having decided to start and begun to think about planning, a teacher has next to embark upon the planning itself, either alone or in concert with willing colleagues. As suggested in section 2.2, the first piece of new planning is likely to represent a departure from existing practice that is not too radical, partly in order to keep the actual exercise of re-planning within manageable limits and partly in order to introduce the children themselves gradually to new ways of working.

One difficulty is to find enough time to do it. Repeatedly, during the schools and diffusion programmes, teachers complained to the Team that they had no time for adequate planning[5]. When starting a new venture, this difficulty is likely to be at its height, but it should be encouraging to teachers to know that other teachers usually found ways of setting aside time to plan and that in one or two schools where teachers were collaborating, small allocations of time were specifically made within the time-table for this purpose.

There still remains, of course, the time required in the

actual preparation and in the methods of assessment which the Project recommends[6]. Especially at first, while teachers are becoming accustomed to its use, this can make considerable demands additional to those involved in hunting out and mobilising material, even though the time spent on preparation and marking of a conventional kind is often much greater than it need be. So it is probably unwise to start the first venture at a time when other pressures are particularly heavy. On the other hand, there is little incentive to change at all when everything is running smoothly. Perhaps the best time to start is when some substantial change is in any case impending such as the introduction of mixed-ability teaching or a change in accommodation but when the staff is stable enough to face that change with confidence. For then, curricular change may be seen as a necessary consequence and may thus be viewed more favourably, while the means exist of carrying it out successfully.

These considerations may sound very obvious but they are necessary to a realistic estimate of what can be done. Once they have been met, then even an individual teacher can begin to try out the feasibility of his planning and then, having adjusted accordingly, to plan more ambitiously, involving a longer time-span and questions of sequence (section 2.4).

One further kind of planning can follow when the innovation is firmly established. Sooner or later, the point will be reached at which there is a dearth of existing material, even when supplemented by the Project's publications, for teachers to incorporate and for children to use. This is the stage at which some familiarity with the disciplines as resources becomes essential, and it is also the stage at which first-hand contact with the disciplines can be particularly stimulating, perhaps even serving to counteract any lassitude or frustration that may have arisen in the earlier stages. The compiling of extracts from relevant original material, the making of slides and tapes, even the act of taking a camera out (with some children) to take photographs illustrating a theme with carefully-selected examples, can engender zest in a quite remarkable way. However, this too takes time and it also requires some degree of advice and help from colleagues and others whose own physical skills for these purposes are well developed, if these new original resources are not to be unduly limited to verbal content.

Some difficulties
Most teachers, having read thus far, will see for themselves difficulties that initiatives of this kind might raise in their own situations. From the Project's experience, some of these could arise rather frequently. One such difficulty arises when a teacher is transferred from one role to another within a school, or moves to another school: the loss of an enthusiastic archaeologist is not compensated, within the social subjects, by the arrival of somebody anxious to establish a brass band. But even if the personnel remains unaltered, an innovation in curriculum planning may simply run out of steam. During the diffusion phase, the Project Team observed this more than once and, having decided against intervention, watched to see what would be the most effective means by which a venture in a school could revive itself. Provided that one or two individuals remained committed to the Project's ideas, a renewal of interest usually followed when the period of intense overpressure and comparative disillusionment was over, simply because teachers who have once shown the initiative required to launch a piece of effective curriculum design are likely, when circumstances are propitious, to produce another, different, but equally good, or better.

Team planning
The maintenance of a momentum in planning, capable of surviving the vicissitudes of staff mobility and collective fatigue, can be substantially helped when a group of teachers develops into a planning team. This can also lead to a more economical use of resources and to a beneficial pooling of ideas; perhaps even to a recognition that the process of planning is of some importance within the school. One such team was established to develop a combined course in one of the Project's comprehensive schools and these comments, reproduced with the permission of a member of the team, may help to illustrate the value of this kind of organisation.

'Initially, co-operation between subject departments was difficult because it involved bringing together a number of departments who had their own ideas about how their subject should be integrated into this type of programme. Each teacher was concerned that the programmes contained enough of his particular subject, i.e. that the Romans, for example, were not just taught from an historical point of view but geography, drama, creative writing etc. were also included. This approach did not work . . .

After these early failures we decided, at an end of term meeting, that the whole course and our attitudes towards it had to be radically changed. We agreed to "bury the hatchet" as far as making sure there was enough English or history etc. in the programmes . . . We began to see the many ways of approaching aspects of work on our community. The community could be looked at from the historical, geographical, sociological, anthropological etc. aspects and all these approaches seemed to complement each other. This also applied to other communities and societies of our country and the world. This seemed to be a far more subtle and meaningful way of approaching the subjects for both staff and pupils'.

In other schools, planning teams included teachers with particular interest in other parts of the curriculum: the visual arts, movement, *Science 5/13*. Where a range of interests can be involved, this not only widens the basis of recognition and support but also suggests ways in which the repertoire of approaches can be extended. Where other projects are established, the sharing of ideas should be beneficial, and certainly not burdensome, since they share the quest for improved ways of learning. However, this is not always easy to achieve. Even within the Project's own schools, there were apparently members of staff who were only dimly, if at all, aware of the Project's existence.

Where heads were fully committed to the Project, however, such ignorance was rarely found. Moreover, the active support of a head can lead to another important way of underwriting curriculum planning in the social subjects, namely the designation of staff posts for responsibility in this field. Such developments have been quite widely pursued in the wake of projects in science and mathematics and if the social subjects are to receive fair treatment and esteem, the same should be done for them.

It will be noticed that the sort of team planning that has been mentioned does not necessarily imply team *teaching*. But this, too, may well be considered. In several junior and middle schools it was practised during the Project's schools programme. It does not necessarily involve what has come to be the usual kind of team teaching[7] with a lead lesson followed by a breakdown into group and individual work. What it does mean is that two or three teachers and classes with a block of time on the time-table should be involved in one unit and that there should be free movement between and outside the rooms, as far as the children, teachers, school and environment render this feasible.

A wider range of support
A further aspect of collaboration within schools relates to work with children below 8, or over 13. Continuity of this kind must be considered on practical grounds alone, but it is educationally important too: the middle years cannot be considered in isolation. Moreover schools involved in, for example, *Geography 14–18*; *Geography for the young school leaver*, or *History 13–16*, as well as the Humanities Project and Keele Integrated Studies, have had to consider how one project can be related to another within a school.

In addition to help from colleagues, teachers can look to sources outside the school. An obvious one, used less in English education than it might be, consists of teachers in other schools. English teachers appear rather reluctant to share ideas in this way, partly through a sense of copyright but partly, too, because English education encourages those who succeed to worry about what they are found out getting wrong rather than to share with others what they get right. (Perhaps we all tend to go through life with our forearm curled metaphorically round our work, as we did when we ourselves were eight years old.)

However, things are changing and it is likely that host schools and teachers' centres will increasingly provide the facilities for fruitful co-operation between teachers, as they have done in many places during the diffusion programme.

The Project's own experience also indicates how institutes of higher education, particularly Colleges of Education, can be involved both through the provision of material facilities and through the specific help given by members of staff (section 3.2). Similarly, public libraries, museums and art galleries should be regarded as important sources of support, usually given with remarkable generosity.

Here and there, too, local curriculum ventures directly relevant to the social subjects have already been launched. The Project's own work in Liverpool benefited through contact with the Educational Priority Area Project formerly directed by Dr. Eric Midwinter[8] and also his other concern, the Liverpool Teachers' Centre, which was associated with the development of the Childwall Project materials[9] and later also with schemes of work directed towards the middle years. When the diffusion phase was launched, other existing local initiatives were encountered, for example in Dudley, Manchester and Southampton; others were established as a part of the diffusion programme itself.

In contrast to these various forms of professional assistance, the lay members of society can also help. For example, in section 1.3 it was pointed out that there are many matters important in a study of Man in Place, Time and Society that lie outside the scope of the social disciplines as such, or even of the social subjects, but which when considered in the light of the social disciplines can be of great value in teaching. Craftsmen, shopkeepers, seamen, bargees, construction workers and planning officials are examples of people who could offer a great deal to a school, if opportunities could be found and permission given, for them to do so. What they often cannot do is to teach; but this gives the teacher a new facet to his own role in mediating their expertise to children, just as he mediates the disciplines themselves (see section 1.3, p. 35). But of course there are some laymen who have 'a way with' children and can, in this limited function, impress teachers by the effectiveness with which they can communicate. A special kind of value attaches here to retired people, for not only does their potential for helping to illustrate continuity/change extend over a longer period than that of any teacher, but they often have the time and sufficient energy to be able to help in a way in which they can feel genuinely useful, as they do when looking after their own grandchildren[10]. It can even be possible to formalise such links through the machinery of Adult Education as suggested in section 3.3. Whatever use is made of outside help, it does of course, make demands on teachers' professional skills and diplomacy both towards their colleagues and towards the outside individuals and groups themselves. However, this is likely to become part of the 'extended' role which Hoyle envisages for teachers in the future[11].

A 'movement' model of diffusion

One final comment of a more general nature must be made about the way in which the Project regards the efforts of teachers, individually and in groups, to maintain innovation in schools. It exemplifies in its way what Donald Schon has called a 'movement' model for the diffusion of ideas[12] in which an initiative, once launched, is left to develop like ripples on a pool when the waters are disturbed by a stone. In fact, there is rarely only one stone and one set of ripples, but a series of related ideas which, in the case of a project, can be taken up and reformulated as a recognisable whole. He proposed this as an alternative to what he called a 'centre-periphery' model in which, in one way or another, ideas were spread in a controlled dissemination from a centre and absorbed at the periphery.

In curriculum development, the 'centre-periphery' model, either intact or in its variant which Schon termed 'proliferation of centres', has almost always been proposed. A central initiative has been taken, through the setting up of a temporary system[13] such as a project team, and then deliberate dissemination has been pursued. This is either through the publication of a standard course[14] or through the establishment of local administrative surveillance[15], or through the running of courses intended to initiate teachers in the handling of specific procedures whose use is regarded as fundamental to the project's strategy[16]. This Project has taken a different view. Where others have trusted to a nationally organised system of dissemination, the Project Team has produced publications, made contacts in a few areas, watched to see in detail how these developed, and for the rest left its ideas and other similar ideas to grow and spread. In doing so, the Project has not simply explored an alternative kind of diffusion. Rather, it has followed what appears to be the usual way in which developments in education actually seem to take place.

It may be that, in opting for this pattern of diffusion, the Project will earn less public notice than those who follow some form of the centre-periphery model. There is an element of risk, for the Project's ideas might be radically altered or lost without trace as the 'movement' develops. However, the experience of the Team in monitoring the diffusion programme suggests that total transformation or oblivion is unlikely. The actual outcome may well be a patchwork across the country in which some places are more closely involved than others in curriculum planning for the social subjects in the middle years, and some show much more direct influence from the Project than others. This uneven distribution should not be regarded as unsatisfactory, provided that it arises from the deep, systematic, reflective thinking on which the Project lays its greatest emphasis. That is genuine curriculum planning, for its growing-points are in the schools themselves[17].

References
1 Hoyle, E. 'How does the curriculum change? (II) Systems and strategies'. *Journal of Curriculum Studies* 1, 3, 1969, especially p. 231.

2 It must be emphasised that the re-thinking which lies at the heart of the Project's ideas can be, and often is, initiated and extended by contact with the many other developments in the social subjects which have been conducted in recent years. The Project's own publications have been designed with a view to guiding planning and supplementing existing resources, not supplanting them.

3 Paper prepared for a Project conference at Homerton College, Cambridge, April 1973.

4 There is now a considerable technical literature on this topic, and increasingly courses are being designed too. A useful introduction is given in Hoyle, E. 'Planned organisational change in education'. *Research in Education* 3, 1, May 1970. For a distinctive and unvarnished account of innovation in one school, which may suggest ideas about what could happen elsewhere, see Richardson, Elizabeth, *The Teacher, the School and the Task of Management.* London, Heinemann, 1973. Another useful indication of the different kinds of impact that a project can make in differing circumstances can be found in Rennie, J., Lunzer, E. A., and Williams, W. T. *Social Education: An Experiment in Four Secondary Schools.* Schools Council Working Paper No. 51. London, Evans/Methuen Educational, 1974, especially Chapter III.

5 See also Baranowski, M. *Pilgrim's Progress through the Project.* Occasional Publication No. 2. Liverpool, Schools Council Project *History, Geography and Social Science 8–13,* 1975.

6 For this purpose see the Project's specific publication by Cooper, K. R. on *Evaluation, Assessment and Record Keeping.*

7 For a thorough survey of team teaching as such, with an emphasis on secondary schools, see Freeman, J. *Team Teaching in Britain.* London, Ward Lock Educational, 1969. Further suggestions, with still greater emphasis on secondary schools, are given in Warwick, D. *Team Teaching.* London, University of London Press, 1971. An interesting recent study of team teaching in junior schools is given by Frank Plimmer in Part 2 of Taylor, Monica (ed.) *Team Teaching Experiments.* Slough, N.F.E.R. 1974.

8 For a general introduction see Midwinter, E. C. *Priority Education.* Harmondsworth, Penguin Books, 1972.

9 This project produced a series of units published by E. J. Arnold and Son Ltd. Leeds.

10 One of the Project's units, based on experience during the schools programme, made specific use of one old lady's

recollections of the school locality. See the Teachers' Guide to *Shops*. Old people's memories are also used in other units notably *Life in the 1930's*.

11 Hoyle, E. 'Strategies of curriculum change' in Watkins, A. R. (ed.) *In-Service Training*. London, Ward Lock Educational, 1973, and 'Professionality, professionalism and control in teaching'. *London Educational Review*, Vol. No. 2. Summer, 1974, pp. 13–19.

12 Schon, D. *Beyond the Stable State: Public and Private Learning in a Changing Society*. London, Temple Smith, 1971 (The Reith Lectures for 1970).

13 This is an idea to which considerable attention has been paid. See for example Miles, M. B. 'On temporary systems', Chapter 19 in Miles, M. B. (ed.) *Innovation in Education*. New York, Bureau of Publications, Teachers College, Columbia, 1964.

14 This has been the characteristic mode of proceeding in science and modern languages.

15 For example, the use of local co-ordinators by *Science 5/13*.

16 The best-known instance is probably the training of teachers for the neutral-chairman role in the Humanities Curriculum Project.

17 One project which has adopted a somewhat similar approach is the North West Curriculum Development Project directed by Dr. Allan Rudd at the University of Manchester School of Education. See Rudd, W. A. 'Teachers as curriculum developers: a second-generation viewpoint' in Taylor, P. H. and Walton, Jack, *The Curriculum: Research, Innovation and Change*. London, Ward Lock Educational, 1974, pp. 52–64.

3.2 Maintaining planning through teacher education

A second kind of impetus is given to any process of curriculum innovation through the system of teacher education. It operates both in the initial training of teachers and in the various forms of professional activity and mutual assistance that can be collectively described as in-service education of teachers.

Each of these will be considered in turn.

Initial training

The Project Team was not able to develop as much work as had originally been hoped with students in initial training, but their general contacts with the University of Liverpool School of Education and with Colleges of Education locally and elsewhere led them to formulate some provisional ideas about the ways in which work in the social disciplines and preparation for teaching the social subjects might be developed. There was certainly no lack of enquiries about the part that Colleges and Departments of Education might play: this makes it all the more important to emphasise that the following suggestions are tentative.

First, the Project's own publications and those of other projects in the social subjects might be studied, both for themselves and for the ideas to which they could give rise. Examples of other related projects for this purpose would be *Environmental Studies 5–13, Keele Integrated Studies, Geography for the Young School Leaver, History 13–16*, and (in considerable contrast) *Man: A Course of Study*. (M.A.C.O.S., now more often just called MAN)[1]. How this can be done in a particular College must depend on organisation and relationships within the college for this, too, represents a variable.

From an examination of the actual materials from a project, students could be led effectively to the exploration of disciplines as resources. This applies in particular to the Social Sciences, which are likely to be least well known to students. A specific introduction to the Social Sciences could well be introduced into the college course especially for students already concentrating on History and Geography; but at the very least they should be encouraged regularly to use the areas of the college library devoted to the disciplines of Economics, Sociology, Social Psychology, Anthropology and Political Science when planning their work.

166

Meanwhile, opportunities should be made available for students to take some part in ongoing schemes of work in schools and elsewhere. Indeed, this would be a mutually beneficial process. Students would gain experience in a fairly protected situation before trying their hand in a more responsible situation, while the schools would gain from the additional help that they could give. This is a situation in which the use of team teaching in the fuller sense is particularly helpful, since senior and junior staff members, students, and college lecturers could all play some part, rather as members of a medical team do, from consultant to student nurse.

Meanwhile, students can and should have a chance of handling the Project's contributions to 'method', such as games and simulations and the kinds of questioning discussed in section 2.3. Discussion of these will go a considerable way towards convincing students of the complexity and stimulus implicit in the handling of the social subjects. It may also help them to sort out their own ideas, and to appreciate that these ideas will go on and on developing but, like the children's own ideas, will never attain finality. And if they have worked carefully with the materials themselves, and have taken the first steps professionally towards thinking deeply, systematically and reflectively about the strategy of a project, then students should be able to begin making a considered criticism of projects as a part of their professional preparation for a wider role.

The incorporation of work of this nature into a college curriculum might even help in the revision of college curricula themselves. For the consideration of the disciplines as resources, as well as systems of enquiry and bodies of knowledge, could lead to a new relationship between the specialists in the disciplines and the 'Education' staff whose prime interest is in schools and the role of subjects in school[2]. At the same time, the use of disciplines as resources could also be relevant to the 'diversified' courses that are to be developed when colleges begin to undertake functions other than the training of teachers. But it must be emphasised that this is only speculation and is not grounded in the Project's experience.

In-service education

If teachers are to be fully professional in their approach to Man in Place, Time and Society for the middle years, then the most important kind of in-service education is the kind discussed in section 3.1, in which they actually work together planning curriculum, and to which, as indicated in the previous part of this section, they introduce students in training. But as in any other profession, there are also specialised agencies which cater for further professional training of one sort or another. *Colleges and Departments of Education* are the most prominent of these agencies. Being located in one of them, and having observed at first-hand the outcome of ventures of different kinds, the Project Team considers that major courses in curriculum development, with a rigorous theoretical and research base combined with direct practical involvement, are of much more value than short courses and it appears likely that, this will be the way in which the potential leaders of curriculum planning within schools will extend their own professional qualifications.

There is a further way in which the staff of colleges, Departments and Schools of Education can assist individually in the maintenance of curriculum developments through in-service activities and this is through participating in groups of teachers and offering specialist advice and help, as far as exigencies of time-tabling and staff mobility permit. One of the most encouraging aspects of the diffusion programme was the way in which individual college staff members gained acceptance among teachers and used their own somewhat more flexible time budgets and library resources in the planning process. (See section 3.1.) They also went into schools to help with the actual teaching and in this way did more than, perhaps, they realised to promote positive relationships between schools and colleges. Moreover, by taking their own students into schools with them, they have taken a step towards the team approach previously discussed. The incorporation into the same team of students in their induction year could be a further useful step. In times of penury in education experiments of this kind are not only encouraging but they actually economise effort, as well as producing a more desirable long-term outcome.

A second agency for in-service training is the *teachers' centre*. There are so many ways in which teachers' centres can be involved in in-service work that it is difficult to generalise about them but it is evident, from the Project's experience of working with a number of centres, that they can and do play an important part in the maintenance of curriculum planning. It is not, however, through the mounting of courses or occasional lectures so much as through the systematic promotion of workshops and other activities among teachers that constructive development can take place. The promotion of these activities obviously places considerable responsibilities on the warden of a centre. He has to be aware both of the needs and capabilities of the teachers who attend, and of the ways in which curriculum planning is being conducted elsewhere. He also has to deploy the support facilities that are required for the making of actual banks of teaching material and cater to some extent for the teachers' need for access to the disciplines as resources. The Team have been impressed by the versatility and inventiveness that is needed in a warden, and have learned a great deal from the wardens who have taken part in the diffusion programme[3].

Finally, a brief reference must be made to *professional associations* which provide, for many teachers, a major means of in-service development. Some of these could more accurately be described as teachers' unions, but it is important to remember that they take very considerable interest in curriculum development, not least because of the part that curriculum improvement can play in the enhancement of professional status. But in addition there are the various subject associations, which enlist the support of many teachers with a subject-orientation. All of the relevant associations have had national, and local, contact with the Project and a number of their branches have been involved in specific attempts to launch and sponsor local initiatives. Each of these organisations is useful as a guide to its own discipline, and membership of a local or regional branch can be very helpful to a teacher seeking to widen his perspective on a discipline. A list of the major associations for the disciplines is given at the end of this section[4].

References

1 *Schools Council Environmental Studies Project: A Teacher's Guide.* London, Rupert Hart-Davis, 1972, and associated publications from the project team directed by M. I. Harris (who was a member of the Project's Consultative Committee – see Appendix IV); *Exploration Man: An Introduction to Integrated Studies.* London, Schools Council Publications/ Oxford University Press, 1972.

(Also Shipman, M. D. with Bolam, D. and Jenkins, D. *Inside a Curriculum Project.* London, Methuen, 1974, which gives a project-centred view of a project); Rudduck, Jean, 'Man: a course of study'. *Cambridge Journal of Education* 2.2, Easter 1972, pp. 118–126. The English 'agent' for the M.A.C.O.S. materials, which are costly but magnificently produced and which embody the essential idea of Bruner's 'spiral curriculum' as they were elaborated for children aged 10–11, is the Centre for Applied Research in Education in the University of East Anglia, where Jean Rudduck is investigating their potentiality for English schools.

2 An interesting suggestion incorporating the use of objectives by and with students is given in Gunning, D. and S. 'Some considerations on professional studies courses in the new B.Ed. degree, with reference to History and Social Studies in the primary school'. *Education for Teaching*, 95, Autumn 1974, pp. 51–59.

3 For a racy general introduction to the work of teachers' centres see Thornbury, R. (ed.) *Teachers' Centres.* London, Longman Darton and Todd, 1973. For a more specific reference to the place that teachers' centres might occupy in curriculum planning, see *Teachers' Centres and the Changing Curriculum.* Schools Council Pamphlet No. 6. London, Schools Council Publications, 1970.

4 The principal associations and their national addresses are:

Geographical Association: 343, Fulwood Road, Sheffield, S10 3BP.

Historical Association: 59A, Kennington Park Road, London, SE11 4JH.

Association for the Teaching of the Social Sciences: Secretary: Ian Shelton, Didsbury College of Education, Manchester, M20 8RR.

Association for the Teaching of Psychology: c/o The British Psychological Association, 18–19, Albemarle Street, London, W1X 4DN.

The Economics Association: Room 340, Hamilton House, Mabledon Place, London, WC1H 9BH.

The Politics Association: 12, Gower Street, London, WC1.

Royal Anthropological Institute: 36, Craven Street, London, WC2N 5NG.

3.3 Maintaining planning through administrative support

General issues

If a 'movement' model of curriculum planning and diffusion is followed, then there is no place for the sort of national network that some projects have set up. Therefore it is hoped that each Local Education Authority will make arrangements appropriate to its own needs but that at the level of administrative support, as in the schools, the needs of the social subjects will be adequately met, in terms both of re-thinking and of resources.

This has not always been the case. Resources, especially of expensive equipment and of ancillary personnel, have been allocated to other parts of the curriculum much more readily than to the social subjects and this has happened partly because in many cases there was nobody near to the centres of decision-making to establish a claim for the social subjects. Indeed, the outcome of projects in other subject-areas has tended to reinforce this imparity since advisory and other staff have sometimes been appointed to ensure their continuing impact, while no comparable appointments have been made until recently for the social subjects.

Equally important is the ensuring of parity as between younger and older children. The Project's approach requires adequate equipment for children under eleven and if this can only be achieved by some redistribution of the budget, then this should be seriously considered.

In this connection it should, however, be appreciated that the innovations proposed by the Project are not unreasonably costly. Much can be done with what schools already have, provided that they have the opportunity to make the best use of it. When teachers collaborate, within or between schools or in teachers' centres, there can be an actual saving in capital outlay, and even in consumables, since the planning and the making of banks of information and of devices such as games and simulations can then be concentrated in one or two places, except in scattered rural areas whose particular problems require in this, as in so many other ways, special consideration.

Examples from the Project's experience
These are a few of the general points that have arisen during the Project's schools and diffusion programmes. It is scarcely possible or appropriate to suggest here, in any comprehensive way, how they can be taken into account by administrators since Local Education Authorities, too, vary and in any case the Project Team do not possess the kind of administrative experience that is required for this purpose. However, some of the particular experiences of the Project may help to indicate what is possible.

For example, two L.E.A.'s made specific allocation of funds for work in the social subjects to the schools in which the Project was based. In one case this took the form of equipment; in the other, there was a choice between an increase in technician support and a slight supplementation of the teaching strength. Not surprisingly, the school opted for the second. In other cases there was virtually no additional material support but the very fact that the administration looked with interest at what was going on itself improved the teachers' morale, while their interest also led them to support decisions about timing introduced within schools, for example the allocation of blocks of time, including planning time, for the social subjects in one middle school.

It was generally easier for administrators to take positive action in respect of provision outside schools. Teachers' centres, for example, were vigorously used and it appeared that the most effective outcome was achieved when a representative of the administration appeared formally to inaugurate a workshop conducted by the Team, or by experienced teachers, and thereafter kept a general eye on developments. (In some cases contact was maintained in a much closer way, because the administrator concerned happened also to be particularly interested in the social subjects: but general administrative duties do not always permit this degree of personal involvement.) Where other projects such as *Geography for the young school leaver* were simultaneously considered, the mutual advantage to both was evident. Since this is likely to be a usual situation in future, concerted planning for groups of projects is virtually necessary.

A particular comment is necessary about the problems of rural areas in planning work of this kind. For on the one hand, it is more difficult for teachers to get to the teachers' centre or indeed to any other point, while on the other, it is particularly important that the resources of small schools in both equipment and personnel should be reinforced by contact with others. The Project actually worked in three rural areas, one of which was particularly sparsely populated, and it appeared necessary in that case to concentrate on regular, but infrequent, meetings in centrally-placed secondary schools, supplemented by correspondence and the telephone. In these circumstances it was surprising how much was achieved, and with what a high measure of skill and interest. (Unfortunately the costs in travel, telephone and correspondence cannot be ignored.) In the same context it might be added that city areas also have problems of access to teachers' centres owing to traffic congestion and similar issues, though they do not of course find the same difficulties in linking schools.

Perhaps the most important issue to emerge from the Project's diffusion trials, from the administrator's point of view, is the question of responsibility for maintaining the momentum of the Project itself. This is the crux of the 'movement' approach. For if there is no central machinery impelling a local organisation to sustain the impetus of an innovation, then either some effective substitute must be found, or the innovation will wither. It is quite easy to see why projects which follow the centre-periphery model exercise an appeal to administrators, because they come with a recognisable set of procedures and perhaps a kit, and the remaining task appears to be only one of organisation and propagation. This Project, instead, calls for a continuing process of curriculum planning and innovation which, the Team believes, will be more effective and durable in practice. The problem is to find some means of keeping this process going and for this purpose it seems that someone has to act as a *sponsor* for the Project and its sequel. This implies finding a member of the administration sufficiently senior to be able to exercise substantial influence in higher-level decision-making.

This higher-level sponsor may well in turn depend for his effectiveness on the initiative and impact of another person at an intermediate level who can be called a *co-ordinator*. One of the first functions of the sponsor should be to find a co-ordinator (or several). This may be an enthusiastic head, a knowledgeable and experienced senior member of staff, a keen young teacher, a warden of a teachers' centre, a lecturer in an institution of higher education, a tutor in adult education, a community worker, a librarian, an archivist, a curator, or indeed anyone who is able and willing to share relevant professional expertise with colleagues and to be responsible for taking initiatives in keeping the process of curriculum planning going. The Project has met examples of most of these during its own activities; all of them have figured in the experience of the Team either during the Project or otherwise. The notion of the local co-ordinator, based to some extent on the procedures developed by *Science 5/13*, was introduced by the Project during the diffusion phase, particularly in those areas in which only minimal contact was maintained, and developed at a conference held in Liverpool. It has become clear that this role, together with that of the sponsor, has proved both viable and useful.

Collaboration between a sponsor and a co-ordinator may therefore be put forward as a promising means of promoting curriculum planning. Of course, like team planning within schools, it is not always proof against hazards and in particular the mobility of teachers and the many other claims on their time and energy. Doldrum phases occur among teachers' groups in teachers' centres and elsewhere and it appears that the most effective way of maintaining the impetus during such phases is to concentrate on some limited but purposive activity, such as a teachers' workshop established to prepare themes and units and support materials for particular schools. Activities of this kind can engender a very real sense of achievement and co-operation among a loyal core of teachers and can thus keep the collective machinery for curriculum planning in being until more general enthusiasm revives.

Some additional suggestions
From their general experience, the Project Team can make a few other specific suggestions which, though not actually tried out during the schools or diffusion programme, seem likely to be helpful.
1 There should be regular, and officially-supported, provision within a school's programme for teachers to have time to plan and to make materials, even if this should mean that the teacher's day has to be different in length from the children's day.
2 There should be some facilitation of co-operation between teachers of younger and of older children, in order to secure increased sharing of expertise and outlook in the teaching of the social subjects (and otherwise) between teachers with different roles. Nowadays, partly owing to the introduction of middle schools, this is happening more frequently than it once did. However, it is also vital to sustain co-operation with teachers of children below 8 and above 13.
3 School programmes could be planned to interact more directly with adult education and community education, so that lay involvement in the education of young children through the provision of special knowledge and expertise, suggested in section 3.1, might be facilitated. This is a more positive means of doing so than the ones that the de-schoolers usually suggest.
4 As mentioned in section 3.1, the designation of posts of responsibility for the oversight of the social subjects

within schools could be actively encouraged by the administration. Although such forms of designation are the prerogative of heads, it is helpful if the Local Education Authority makes it known that a policy of this kind would be viewed with favour. It is not, of course, suggested that the social subjects should have preferential treatment; only parity.

5 Finally, it is worth emphasising that Local Education Authorities can do much for the morale of teachers of the social subjects if they show openly that these subjects are not a low-priority area in the curriculum. The selection of schools for visits by distinguished guests; references to the social subjects in public statements; inclusion of this area of the curriculum in programmes of lectures and courses: these are some ways in which official interest can be expressed and the Project Team were delighted to see how those L.E.A.'s which co-operated with the Project itself (appendix 3) were able to display their own concern about the introduction of children to Place, Time and Society.

3.4 Conclusion

The process of curriculum planning, which this book is intended to promote, is one that has a beginning but no end. Teachers, administrators and others involved in the educational process will continue to make decisions and to allocate resources of time and money, and there will never be enough of either. However, the Project has been launched during times of scarcity and has shown that scarcity is no deterrent to enthusiasm. It is hoped that the Project's experience, as embodied in this book, will help others in their turn to channel their own enthusiasm into the effective planning of curriculum.

Now that their task is almost completed the Project Team feel that they are nearer the beginning than the end. As the Project proceeded they came to appreciate, more vividly, the range and challenge of their responsibility and the extent of the intellectual excitement and the social engagement which it involves. This challenge is now for others to take up, for there is still an immense amount to be done.

One aspect of the incompleteness of the Team's task does, however, call for particular emphasis; the Project Team would have been much happier if more of their suggestions had been based on sound and thorough research. Their location in a University School of Education, and the constructive comments of their colleagues, served to remind them constantly that they were making assertions for which the evidence was less strong than they would have wished. In fact they could easily have spent the whole of their four years' effort in applying research to the problems involved; instead, they had to be in action alongside teachers and administrators who were grappling with those problems all the time. Fortunately, especially in the field of advanced study and of in-service education discussed in section 3.2, there is plenty of opportunity still for others to do what the Team could not, and in particular for the systematic study of problems such as these:

The nature of key concepts, and their epistemological and psychological significance.[1]

How children form and attain particular concepts in the social subjects.

How children respond to a series of curricular innovations in the social subjects over the years between 5 and 18.

The bases on which decisions about the sequencing of themes can be justified, between 8 and 13 but also more generally.

How teachers can appraise their own professional capacities to undertake innovation in the curriculum.

How innovations are carried out in particular schools, especially middle schools.

How student teachers in initial training can be introduced to the use of objectives and key concepts in curriculum planning.

How modifications in the teacher's role, and in the organisation of schools, could promote the planning of curriculum.

How teachers who are relatively familiar with none, or with only one of the social disciplines can acquire facility in the others and use this in teaching the social subjects.

It is now for the Team and others to take up the challenge

and to explore these important questions so that their findings too can contribute to the never-ending programme of curriculum planning.

In the Introduction, the Project placed its faith firmly in the approach to curriculum development that begins from the unique situation. Everything that has been said about the disciplines as resources in interrelation, about themes, about objectives and their implementation through key concepts, about actual procedures, sequencing, assessment, and the maintenance of the momentum of planning has been set against that basic assumption. All of it really centres on the second of the four variables in each unique situation, namely the teachers. It is their professional development which the Project seeks to promote and assist. For their growth carries with it the promise of purposive growth for the children, development for the schools, and a social process leading to the improvement of their physical and social environments.

The Project also has a set of values and these too have been sustained all the way through. They belong to a certain kind of democracy which respects the unique situation and which sets great store upon critical thinking, empathy and autonomy, as well as perhaps a vision of excellence.

If the unique situation, and the unique people who grow up in it, can be improved through the implementation of those values, the Project will be well satisfied. Meanwhile, as we all look towards the unknown region of 2000 or 2010 in which children now in their middle years of schooling will have to live, feel, believe, adjust and make decisions, the Project can do no more than offer them the best approach it knows to Man in Place, Time and Society. We must all hope that their experiences in school now and in the next decade will help them in due course to live in that world more wisely. Some of us may be there to see whether they do.

Reference

1 See Kingdom, Elizabeth F., *Key Concepts and Curriculum Planning*. Occasional Publication No. 3, Liverpool, Schools Council Project *History, Geography and Social Science 8–13*, 1975 and for a different perspective, Holly D., *Beyond Curriculum*, London, Hart-Davis, MacGibbon, 1973.

Appendixes

Appendix one – some useful references on the teaching of the social subjects

It is not practicable to include an extensive bibliography in the present volume. The following is a list of particularly relevant books related to the teaching of the social subjects. These books include bibliographies of their own which can be followed up by teachers and others who want to study a particular topic.

Geography

Bailey, P. *Teaching Geography*. Newton Abbot, David and Charles, 1975.

Bale, J., Graves, N. and Walford, R. (eds.) *Perspectives in Geographical Education*. Edinburgh, Oliver and Boyd, 1974.

Graves, N. *Geography in Secondary Education*. Sheffield, Geographical Association, 1971.

Long, Molly (ed.) *Handbook for Geography Teachers*. (6th edition) London, Methuen, 1974.

Pemberton, P. *Teaching Geography in Junior Schools*. Sheffield, Geographical Association, 1959.

Walford, R. (ed.) *New Directions in Geography Teaching*. London, Longmans, 1973.

History

Ballard, M. (ed.) *New Movements in the Study and Teaching of History*. London, Temple Smith, 1970.

Burston, W. H. and Green, C. W. (ed.) *Handbook for History Teachers*. (2nd edition) London, Methuen, 1972.

Coltham, J. B. *The Development of Thinking and the Learning of History*. H.A. Pamphlet TH 34. London, Historical Association, 1971.

Jones, R. Ben *Practical Approaches to the New History*. London, Hutchinson Educational, 1973.

Lamont, W. (ed.) *The Realities of History Teaching*. London, Chatto & Windus, 1972.

Mays, Pamela *Why Teach History?* London, University of London Press, 1974.

Watts, D. G. *The Learning of History.* London, Routledge and Kegan Paul, 1972.

Social studies

Fenton, E. *Teaching the New Social Studies in Secondary Schools: An Inductive Approach.* NY, Holt Rinehart & Winston, 1966.

Lawton, D. and Dufour, B. *The New Social Studies: a Handbook for Teachers in Primary, Secondary, and Further Education.* London, Heinemann, 1974.

Mathias, P. *The Teachers' Handbook for Social Studies.* London, Blandford Press, 1974.

Morrissett, I. and Stevens, W. Williams (eds.) *Social Science in the Schools: a search for a rationale.* NY, Holt Rinehart & Winston, 1971.

Sumner, H. 'Economics in Schools: The Case for an Inter-related Approach'. *Economics.* Vol. X. Part 6. Winter 1974. (Journal of the Economics Association.)

Sumner, H. 'Psychology in the School Curriculum'. *The Social Science Teacher.* Vol. 4. No. 2. Winter, 1974. (Journal of the Association for the Teaching of the Social Sciences.)

Vulliamy, G. 'Teaching sociology: a new approach'. *New Society.* 23. (8 Mar. 73) p. 527-9.

Three other useful references

Hammersley, A. D., Jones, E. and Perry, G. A. *Approaches to Environmental Studies.* London, Blandford Press, 1968.

Kelly, A. V. *Teaching Mixed-Ability Classes.* London, Harper and Row, 1974.

Watts, D. G. *Environmental Studies.* London, Routledge and Kegan Paul, 1969.

The introductory handbooks to some other projects such as Environmental Studies 5–13 and Keele Integrated Studies will also be found particularly useful. (Details are available from the Schools Council Information Services.)

Appendix two – some schools involved in the experimental programme

The Project Team wish to record their gratitude to the schools who so readily gave them facilities to develop their ideas, and to the teachers who contributed so much to those ideas. Without these schools, there could have been no Project, and no *Curriculum planning*.

The names of these schools are quoted by permission of the schools themselves and of the Local Education Authorities concerned, without whose co-operation the experimental programme could not have been undertaken. To them also the Project Team wish to express their thanks.

Aldryngton County Primary School, Earley, Reading
Cemaes County Primary School, Cemaes Bay, Anglesey, Gwynedd
Clint County Primary School, Liverpool
Colville Junior School, London W.11
Crewe County Grammar School for Boys, Crewe, Cheshire
Crewe County Grammar School for Girls, Crewe, Cheshire
Gateacre Comprehensive School, Woolton, Liverpool
Gorsedale Middle School, Wallasey, Wirral
Holyrood School, Chard, Somerset (Mixed Comprehensive)
Hunmanby Hall School, Filey, East Yorkshire
Isaac Newton School, London W.10 (Boys' Comprehensive)
Ladbroke School, London W.10 (Girls' Comprehensive)
Llanddeusant County Primary School, Llanddeusant, Anglesey, Gwynedd
Maiden Erlegh School, Earley, Reading (Mixed Comprehensive)
Manor Court County Primary School, Chard, Somerset
Minehead Middle School, Minehead, Somerset
Neroche County Primary School, Broadway, Ilminster, Somerset
Oxford Gardens Junior School, London W.10
Paddington Comprehensive School, Liverpool
Pipworth Middle School, Sheffield
Quarry Mount Middle School, Wallasey, Wirral
Sir Thomas Jones School (Ysgol Gyfyn Syr Thomas Jones),

Amlwch, Anglesey, Gwynedd (Mixed Comprehensive)
St. Lawrence College Junior School, Ramsgate, Kent
St. Swithin's School, Croxteth, Liverpool (Mixed Secondary Modern)
Westways Middle School, Sheffield
Whiteknights County Primary School, Reading
Wistaston Green Junior School, Crewe, Cheshire
Woolton County Primary School (Junior Department), Liverpool

Appendix three – some Local Education Authorities involved in the diffusion programme

Anglesey (Gwynedd)   Liverpool
Cheshire   Manchester
Cumberland (Cumbria)   Sheffield
Derbyshire   Somerset
Inner London   Wallasey (Wirral)
Leeds   Wigan
Lincoln (Lincs)

(Where the Authority's name was changed during the course of the Project, the new name is given in brackets)

These Local Education Authorities have provided facilities of various kinds. Some of them have agreed to accept considerable help from the Project; others have worked with much less direct contact. In this way the Project has been able to explore different patterns of diffusion, and the Project Team must here again record their appreciation of the co-operation that these Authorities have given.

Appendix four – the Project's Consultative Committee

Professor A. M. Ross, Chairman
Miss J. D. Browne, Vice-Chairman

J. Backhouse
Rev. J. R. Carhart
R. Charlton
M. I. Harris
Dr. E. C. Midwinter
B. J. Murphy, M.B.E.
E. E. Newton, M.B.E.

J. S. Nicholson
A. M. S. Poole
S. W. T. Roberts
J. Warren
D. G. Watts
Rev. R. G. Wickham

Representatives of the University of Liverpool
Dr. E. Brooks (since 1973)
M. G. Cook
J. A. Patmore (until 1973)

Schools Council Officers
Curriculum Officers
R. Price
G. Porter, H.M.I.
Miss N. Bartman
T. W. F. Allan, H.M.I.

Publications Department
Miss J. Sturdy
Miss S. LeRoux
Dr. D. Recaldin
Miss B. Rowe

In addition, the Project was helped by a number of other people, some of them designated Consultants, Associates or Local Co-ordinators, who held discussions and conferences with the Team, read parts of manuscripts, and generally gave the benefit of their valuable advice. To all of these, too numerous to be separately listed, the Project owes a debt of gratitude.

Index

evaluation of 147
examinations
external 143
public 70, 139, 140
expressive movement 83

Fenton, Edwin 55
'four variables, the' 13, 39, 70,
88, 104, 108, 126, 131, 141
interaction between 18

Games 45, 56, 167, 172
Geography 27-8, 41-50, 65
concepts in 42
'new' 42-3
as a resource 41, 43, 44-5, 106
skills in 42, 43
Geography for the Young School
Leaver 142, 160, 166, 173
Geography 14-18 160
global perspective 46
graphicacy 46

'Hidden curriculum' 64
History 27, 31, 43, 46, 51-8, 65
engaging pupils' interest in 53
enquiry in 54
evidence in 54
in geography lessons 42
impartiality in writing 56
local 53
people in 55-6
recent 53
as a resource 106
roots in 52-3
studies in children's thinking
in 52
History 13-16 142, 160, 166
Hogben, D. 74
home and homeland 45
Hoyle, E. 153, 162
Human Biology as a resource
106
humanities 28, 29
Humanities Curriculum Project
40, 160
hypotheses 52, 81

Imagination
developing children's 56
sociological 60
indeterminate issues 116
inductive method of learning 65

integrated studies 28, 29, 36-41,
133, 139
intellectual development in
children 73
intellectual skills 85
'higher level' 74, 81, 83
issues 23-7
sensitive 139

Jackson, P. W. 64

Keele Integrated Studies Project
40, 160, 166
key concepts 44, 71, 91-110,
133, 135, 139, 150, 154, 177
differences, coarse and fine
129-31
methodological 95; causes and
consequences 94, 96, 97-8;
continuity/change 53, 94,
96-7; similarity/difference
43, 49, 64, 94, 96
substantive 95; communication
94, 95; conflict/consensus
49, 94, 95; power 94, 95;
values and beliefs 94, 95
and sequence 128-31
use of 98-103

Lawton Report (SC Working
Paper No. 39) 30, 39, 58, 66,
126
laymen, assistance from 161
learning, progression in 114,
127-8
liaison
between colleges of education
and schools 168
in curriculum planning 131
between teachers 175
literary disciplines as a resource,
34
local community 139
local environment 45, 66, 70, 73
local studies 42, 48

McNaughton, A. H. 65
Man: A Course of Study 93, 166
maps and mapwork 42, 43, 78
mediators, teachers as, of
disciplines 35
methods of enquiry 61
Mills, C. W. 60